LEAD

with

VALUE

*How leaders unleash their vision,
empower others, and evolve their business*

KAREEN WALSH

Published by Revampologist, LLC

Printed in the United States of America

First Printing, 2019

ISBN: 978-0-578-43712-5
ebook ISBN: 978-0-578-43713-2

For questions or more information, visit www.kareenwalsh.com

Book cover design, interior design, typesetting, and pre-press production by Lisa Von De Linde, LisaVdesigns.com

DEDICATION

*This book is for the leaders I have learned from;
the leaders I have had the priveldge of working with;
and the leaders who work tierlessly to make every day
better than the day before for themselves,
their organization, and their clients.*

● ● ● ● ● ●

TABLE OF CONTENTS

INTRODUCTION

Ever wonder if leading others could be easier? What if there were fewer personality conflicts and you could engage with your team without feeling like you were herding cats? What if you could create a thriving work environment and lead better by making simple tweaks to your level of awareness and your communication skills?

You can. The first step is to raise your awareness of what you value most and then articulating it to those around you. The second step is to understand the values of those you work with. The third step is to learn how to be a master facilitator to create this environment in each arena you enter.

Leadership requires navigating and leveraging your hired talent, delegating with grace, and having a strong hold on growth and scalability. As a senior executive who has helped leaders launch and build scalable companies, I know that excellence in leadership takes a company further, faster. From my passion for helping individuals to maximize their talent and remove obstacles to build the legacy, reputation, income, and continuous growth they seek, I discovered the one simple practice to enhance each exchange. That is to lead with value.

We can accomplish much by doing, but does that fill us up? No. Leading out of obligation, demand, strength, or necessity creates a burden that evokes our reaction rather than our creativity. Leading from our reactive space may deliver momentary satisfaction for accomplishment of the task at hand, but the long-term effect of this approach is not scalable. It leads to burnout, health issues, feeling alone, and a lack of fulfillment. When you lead with value and understand the value system within which you work, your level of fulfillment rises with each step. Your ability to inspire, motivate, and lead others toward a common goal becomes easier. You create work/life integration because your values apply to both your work and your life. The trade-off of imbalance no longer exists, you are who you are meant to be, and you gracefully leverage the values of others. That is Value Exchange Leadership™ in action.

In this book I share personal stories, client coaching interactions, and best practices to create a Value Exchange Leadership™ stance and environment. In order to make a lasting impression on coworkers, employees, and those whom you lead, you must define your Personal Value System. If you don't know what you value, you can't articulate it. If you can't articulate it, others can't follow and assess if they are a fit in your ecosystem. Imagine how it would feel to articulate your values, assess whether your environment cultivates those values, and understand the values of the people you work with and for. Wait, I want you to reread that last statement, so it sinks in:

Imagine how it would feel to articulate your values, assess whether your environment cultivates those values, and understand the values of the people you work with and for.

When you recognize misalignment of values, you can plan your next move to find the value exchange environment that best matches what you offer.

As a business leader, you are always in the middle. You are between your clients and your team, or between your board and your executives, or between your direct manager and your direct reports. At each interaction, there is an exchange. It can feel like a tug-of-war when the value systems do not align, and you feel depleted if you constantly give away value without receiving value in return. The most effective leaders I engage are holistic thinkers who manage complex environments. Leading in these environments has many moving parts, so it is important to assess the effectiveness of your leadership style in that corporate culture. How you develop your team processes and systems to optimize operations and sustain growth determines your overall effectiveness.

Commonalities exist in the structure of companies of all sizes. As the CEO of my coaching-and-consulting firm, I have engaged with many different leaders who seek the value I bring to teach them how to leverage these methods. I call myself a Growth Strategist, because if you are not personally growing, your bottom line will not sustainably grow, no matter what strategies you put in place. Each company must integrate people, process, and technology in order to thrive. The driving differentiator of all firms is in the talent at the table. Many talented people reach burnout because they are undervalued and don't know how to approach their leaders. If top talent leaves your firm, I guarantee it is due to a misalignment of values and the inability to break through to the next level within your firm. If you question whether the company you are working for is the right fit, the exercises in this book will help you identify the misalignment. If you are a C-Suite leader or founder of your firm and you want to build a company that can withstand any challenge, these methods are for you. If your business growth has been stagnant, it is 100 percent due to the lack of growth across the leadership team. Master first how you lead yourself.

Clients hire me for three main reasons:

1. I don't bullshit about the hard stuff.
2. I help break the unfulfilling cycle of a valueless circumstance across their organization by focusing on what each leader brings to the table.
3. I make sure they accelerate their growth and stop leading with assumption or avoidance—to know without a doubt that as leaders they can build a thriving value-exchange-based organization.

I don't step into these arenas lightly, because I know the impact of working together, and I want to deliver value at every turn.

Lead with Value will help you leverage the tools I share with my leaders, so you can jump into action. The first step in all arenas of my coaching is to identify your leadership vision. If you don't know why you want to be a leader and where you want to make an impact, we won't know how to get you there. I will present important assessment tools to identify your Personal Value System and effectiveness as a leader. We then explore how to facilitate building a Team Value System and an Organizational Value System, so that you can create the environment within which to thrive. These game-changing methods bring clear focus and a communication path that is practical to implement. I've written this book to extend my reach and help you on a growth path to lead with ease, to raise your fulfillment factor, and to optimize the values you bring to the table.

Value Exchange Leadership™ (VXL) principles show you how to grow in all directions. We all want to expertly navigate and accomplish what is in front of us while looking ahead. This book will show you that you are not alone on the journey of a leader in action. Through my book and my VXL programs, I create an environment of inclusion and growth for leaders, so we can impact more lives and show others they are capable of leading.

This book outlines some of my fundamental practices. Your implementation of these practices will set the foundation for the type of leader you want to become, and it will direct your action plan to achieve your ultimate leadership level. I have personally invested more than $150,000 in additional training, seminars, events, and sessions with masterminds to up-level my skill set as a leader and a coach. In my service as an executive and CEO of my own business, I stretched myself and tested what I learned by putting it into action. I decided to leverage the tools I learned, designed, and mastered over time, and I have combined them in this book for your advantage. When you put this into practice, you will grow yourself, and you will help the managers who report to you by sharing these methods with them.

If you are looking to earn a C-Suite position in your career and have not yet achieved it, this book will propel you forward with new facilitation skills to build value-exchange environments and empower your teams to do the same. And if you are currently sitting in a C-Suite position, looking at your firm and your bottom line and wondering why the needle is not moving, or if you are worried about how to withstand a downturn market, you will learn methods to bring all obstacles to the surface and evolve your business to create a continuous growth model that makes you proud.

I kick off this book by sharing some of the Value Exchange Leadership™ work I have done with my clients. It is the easiest way for you to see how these methods work in action. Once you understand the mindset and methodology, you can apply the exercises to your own leadership stance.

Okay, I know your time is valuable. Now that you know my intention for the book, let's jump in.

▶ CHAPTER
One

"What you have to give, you offer

least of all through what you say;

in greater part through what you do;

but in greatest part through who you are."

BOB BURG AND JOHN DAVID MANN, COAUTHORS OF *THE GO-GIVER LEADER*

THE POWER OF THE VALUE EXCHANGE

In a recent coaching session, one of my elite executive clients expressed his desire to become an equity partner in his firm. Up until now, he was a senior executive running a region of the business without a partner equity stake or a title for which he qualified, and he thought it was time to up-level into an ownership role. Prior to engaging me as his coach, he had used his approach and methods to gain a partnership role, but the firm's managing partners still had not granted him the role or recognition that he sought. Before he planned his exit strategy, he wanted to be sure that he had tried everything possible. He knew in his gut that there was a way to make it happen—but he might be limited in how best to approach it.

I thrive when people come to me with a desire to step up and do more to be more. Initially, my clients tend to have one agenda that ultimately leads to the true agenda of how best I can serve them. This leader first asked to better his leadership style and leverage feedback that came back from a 360 review by his current management, peers, and colleagues. We navigated data points and emotions in our first session. The root of the issue he grappled with—his personal agenda to become a partner in his firm, to earn equity, and to be recognized as a true leader of the firm—was not being fully addressed by the company's managing partners. In turn, he felt deflated. He was considering an exit strategy that would likely make him feel as if all his effort to date in a role that was lower than his self-perceived worth had been for nothing. Worst of all, he feared he would have to start all over again.

His tunnel-vision focus on the lack of results he desired had created an imaginary dilemma. My client felt defeated as he recounted the moment to me, and it wasn't only due to the lack of response from the managing partners. It was his awareness of where he was today in relation to his expectation of where he had hoped to be. He felt that by now people should see his greatness and comply with his wishes. After more than thirty years in business and leadership in running his own company, he now wanted to partner with another.

He defined success as ownership, a stake in the business, an equity-return on his time and business-building investment. If he could not achieve that, he felt "less than." He was clear on what he wanted and completely capable of achieving it. He offered substantial value and an agenda he wanted to bring to fruition. Alongside this warranted arrogant stance, he held a desire to be self-aware and conscious of how others received him, and he wanted to be a Servant Leader. He had been a consultant for years and, as such, was generally the expert in the room. He became a coach to increase his impact and leverage the skills to assist others in achieving their goals. Now he realized he wanted to lead again. What he really wanted from the managing partners was recognition and ownership that would give him a return on his efforts to build the business in a region where his managing partners did not have previous experience. That was the value he brought to the table. In our conversation, I helped my client change his perspective of seeing this as a dilemma, I encouraged him to focus on understanding what was valuable to these managing partners and how he could best tell them the ways in which he supported that vision. Through this communication, both sides would immediately feel a greater sense of fulfillment.

In our initial sessions, he described the business structure, the type of personalities he was working with, how they led, the team size, and the company financials. I asked what he had tried so far, so I could better understand the landscape of his business field and know more about the people he wanted to partner with. I asked why he thought he would be a good partner and what he brought to the table. He laid it all out for me in detail.

I also asked how long he had desired to be a managing partner of this region, and I asked what feedback or communication he had received from his managing partners. He said discussions had been in play for over a year, but no decisions had been made. He had laid out a detailed plan for the partnership structure, his equity stake in the business, and how revenue could be shared to make it worthwhile for him to stay with the company. No response. He had leadership team meetings with them, and when he broached the subject, it was deferred to another time. He felt deflated, confused, and led on.

I assessed his side of the story, understood his desire, and focused on his approach thus far. He knew the outcome he wanted, and he had tried everything he could think of. As an outsider looking in, I saw two major items missing. First, it was he—not the managing partners—who initiated the partnership proposal. The partners were unaware that adding him to the managing partner team was even on the table. Second, his approach for his desired outcome did not include a win for the managing partners. Without knowing the benefits of having my client as a managing partner, why would they give up an equity stake? What was the value exchange?

I asked my client, "Before you sent your proposal for partnership, was there a desire by the managing partners to have another partner? Did they open the door, or did you?" "Giving up" a portion of partnership growth and equity shares to someone new feels like relinquishing control. Start your growth and contribution dialogue by showing how all pockets will get fuller with the equity stake, and your acceptance rate will be higher.

I asked, "How do they gain from your helping them grow the business? How are you going to earn your share?" He paused, and it was an "aha" moment. He said that he never laid out how he would help them raise the bar that would earn his share. Instead, he defiantly did less in his current role, as if to say, "Hey, if you are not going to pay me what I want, I am not going to do more than I am asked to do." It was not his true nature, but his defeated stance caused him to rebel when he didn't get the answer he wanted.

I called him out on it. "The mirror is up now. Do you see how your behavior deters them from adding you as partner?" Withdrawing his value from the firm resulted in their devaluing him. I pointed out that the plan he presented showed what his positive outcome would be, but it said nothing about what they would get by adding him on as a partner. "What will you change about what you do today to grow the business in a way that warrants the equity stake? Where is that proposal and what is the timeline for your actions to benefit the whole? What will you need to make that happen? What is the value exchange?"

When you focus on the value exchange in every transaction, both parties win. It is easier to get a *yes* from the other side when you are clear about how they will benefit from the arrangement. My client had proposed no benefits to the business and existing partnership. Why would they consider giving up equity if they could see no upside? I gave him an assignment: Between now and the next session, create a value exchange plan that outlines the wins for the managing partners and his approach to make it happen. Get clear on the value exchange *for both parties*. We knew he wanted equity and ownership, but what would the other partners receive for that stake in the business?

My client's "aha" was realizing that he assumed they understood his value to help them build business in this region, but he had never explained how he would do it and align with the partnership. He now saw how his approach could turn off the partners, so we strategized on how he could approach the next meeting with value exchange as the intention for each proposal on the table.

Value Exchange Leadership™ (VXL) is all about growth through learning. No matter what your level of management, enhance your focus from what *you* have to offer, what *you* desire, what *your* path is. Then add the lens of what the *other persons* (your direct reports, your C-Suite executives, your board members, or your clients) will receive. That's the VXL process.

Update on this Client

On implementing the Value Exchange Leadership™ stance, my client was given an equity partnership stake and is now one of the managing partners in the business. He has increased their regional team and business, because (a) he feels valued and empowered, and (b) he is giving value to his partners by increasing revenue shares and stepping up as a leader and trainer to his team. All of this has resulted in building sustainable clients and raving fans in his market.

A More Common Occurrence

Have you ever been laid off and started to believe that your value in your industry is tarnished? Unfortunately, layoffs are not uncommon across different levels of employment. A layoff can feel confusing to someone who has given so much time and effort to a company, believing he has added value, only to now be let go. How do people navigate something that is completely out of their control, when they feel like they have to scramble to maintain status quo? If you shift your focus on the value you receive to focus on the value of the system you plan to join next, it will help you find a better fit. It will also prepare you with tools in case it happens again.

Consider this specific case that exemplifies how to recover from questioning your value to leveraging a circumstance in order to find your fit and go after what you want. After delivering my "Be A Badass: Six Tools to Up-Level Your Life" online program, one of my badasses asked for one-on-one coaching to navigate her current employment situation. She realized through the program that she wanted to up-level her career and be highly regarded as a Creative Design Leader. She recounted her recent layoff from the agency she was working with, feeling undervalued and questioning what she could have done differently. How could she have sustained a thriving career with this company? She described how she was being led and assigned out to projects, the hours she worked, the level of effort she put in with her clients, their adoration for her, and her success with the projects. In spite of all that, the company fired her without just cause.

I questioned the value system of the firm. The requirements for each project delivery, assignment, and method of engagement with their own employees was inhumane. It did not consider the person behind the work, their bandwidth, or their desire to do great work for the client. This agency focused on throughput, getting paid their margin for each project completed, and moving quickly on to the next. The company valued the bottom line over its team. They valued the ability to call it done over the quality of work that the team could produce, if given the time. They valued younger, hungry grunt workers over senior designers—people whose experience merited more pay due to better results for the firm and their clients. That's the value my client brought to the table, and it was stripped bare when they realized she did not fit the mold and could not churn out the work fast enough for their demands. She focused on quality; they focused on quantity. Their values were not aligned.

My first session was to show her that she had not failed; the system failed her. She had been willing to do whatever it took, and her health suffered for it. She worked overtime without pay.

She lacked excitement about her work, and she was stagnant in her role. She was being taken advantage of and mismanaged. I cheered the fact that she was let go because now she could assess what really mattered to her and figure out what corporate system would fit her best. We worked on rebuilding her bruised ego. (No one likes to be let go.) When you do everything you know and still are not groomed for growth with the company, you naturally feel discarded and undervalued. I assigned actions for her to take between sessions to build herself up, to define what she wanted next, and to identify what to avoid in order not to repeat the same scenario.

She clearly defined the type of company she wanted to be a part of and gained clarity on her ultimate career, and we worked backwards from there to determine her action plan to achieve the next level. We worked on her personal brand for the career she wanted, rather than just selling what she can do. We practiced how she would present herself in conversations with hiring managers and teams to evoke an offer. She followed through on every assignment and put it to the test as she navigated her next career move. She realized that she needed to detox the previous work environment in order not to attract the same situation. As of this writing, she is interviewing with Google and in the final rounds of conversations to confirm that she can thrive in their environment and ensure a value exchange for what she brings to the table and what the company can provide her.

It is easy to fall into the trap of expecting a company to take care of you. You will be groomed. You will grow. Most of all, there is an expectation that someone else will guide you on your path. In most cases, you are left to your own devices. Those who choose to grow beyond their status quo ask for more training, ask for more time with their direct manager, seek out the influencers in the field they want to grow in, and learn from others who have gone before them. The percentage of leaders who have been shown how to build other leaders to increase the value they bring to the table is small. If you plan to lead others, learn to up-level those who report in, so you can move forward in your career. If you plan to grow past your current role, grooming someone else to take your place is the easiest way to move forward.

Be Unapologetically Value-Ridden

I laugh and shake my head at my bold expression to an executive coaching client. This client needed to wake up and face how he was showing up and how to step into his greatness. After only two months of working together, I had helped him identify the gaps in the skill set of his direct reports, the lack of structure and opera-tions across his team, and his need to break old habits of the chief-level staff to make the impact he desired. For him to really step up, make the hard decisions, and get into action was daunting. He was overwhelmed, scared, and excited, all at the same time.

About eight weeks into working together, we had a one-on-one session in his office. It was a typical Manhattan office—grey on grey with a window that looked onto another building right across the street. We had just finished a whiteboarding session where he drew out the layers of service and team structure he envisioned. He was crystal clear about what needed to happen next, but he was unsure how to go about it. He kept focusing on a limiting belief that he should not rock the boat and risk losing his job by proposing his plan to the executive board. He kept saying, "I have only been here six months."

He had voiced this excuse probably ten times, and now he looked down at the floor in fear, almost cowering from the leader-ship life he had stepped into and the potentially amazing impact he could make on the firm if he would just go for it. I saw him hiding from the man I knew he was inside as he played into a toxic leadership environment that had been accustomed to the status quo, not optimizing newer techniques or technology to enhance their customer experience. He was holding back from putting himself out there. He was playing small.

He had a vision of achieving the role he was hired into, but it was a stretch for him now that it was real. Self-doubt crept in once he understood the internal hurdles he would have to overcome to make his desired impact. His Personal Value System was cloudy, and he forgot what he most loves to offer: innovation. He wanted to create new product channels. More than that, he wanted to break the mold and leave his mark at the company and for the company. Now, that is a VXL vision!

I took a deep breath. I stood three feet from him and squared my shoulders to align with his. I looked him straight in the eyes and said, "You have been here six months. Enough already! Balls out, man!" Gasp, did I just say that out loud? I heard my own fearful self-talk: *Shit, this dude is going to fire me! What did I just say?*

Putting all negative thoughts aside, I continued in the zone of this-is-not-about-me and said: "You have been here six months; you know what you need to do to shake things up! You didn't take this job to conform; you took it to challenge yourself and help grow the company. Why are you hiding behind your length of time on the job? You are the leader of this team. Yes, it is challenging, but if it wasn't, you wouldn't feel the growth. You earn this salary for a reason. You were hired for a reason. Balls out, man! You have everything you need to do this. What will make you step into your plan of action? The time is now!"

Silence.

I kept my eyes locked on him, radiating assurance that he had everything he needed to do this. I wish I could have snapped a picture of the change in his stance. He was a little shocked by my word choice, but my point was to shake him out of it, and I did! He stood taller, felt more empowered, and said to give him two weeks until our next check-in. He was ready to push forward and deliver a progress report in our next one-on-one that he could be proud of. It was awesome!

I left his office, shocked that he hadn't fired me. Who says that? I never said that to anyone before, but I trusted it was what he needed now. Thank God it worked. He proceeded to send me to his international and West Coast offices to assess his leadership teams and help him execute a staffing plan that not only has helped drive revenue for the firm but has also built his reputation as a badass in his market. He realized limiting beliefs and inaction had been the only thing stopping him. He needed to build a kick-ass team to align with his plans.

That exchange, where I leveraged a communication skill to shake up the moment and add value to his leadership stance, is one of my favorite value-exchange moments. It energized him to step into his value structure and stop focusing on obstacles.

This client and I have worked together now for four years. I have a no-bullshit, don't-waste-my-time stance regarding getting into action to fulfill your vision for yourself. Some people like it; some run from it. This client continues to lean on my ability to focus on a value-exchange path and share clear ways of communicating it. He has now built a team that aligns with his value-exchange vision. They have all grown in their roles in the firm, and their reputation in the industry is now well-known.

Value Exchange at the Partnership Level

When two founders of a new startup launch and grow their business to over $1.2 million in revenue in their second year of business, you know they offer something solid to their clients. When the CEO of the company hired me after Year One of opening the doors, she was not sure how best to work together, but she knew in her gut that she wanted to do and be more for her team. She realized she was limited in her leadership role and style because she had run only one other company before this one. That was with another family member who had been in business far longer than she had. She loved working with family, but she also felt it was time to take a leadership stance and explore how best to show up for her team and her business partner, who also happened to be her husband.

We started by focusing on her leadership vision, along with the understanding of what it means to be an owner versus an operator of her business. To create a workable vision for the life you want, you need to be clear on the role that will be most fulfilling. Granted, as you learn more and expose yourself to more, your role will change. As I explained to her the benefits of being an owner versus being an operator, she realized she was thinking too small about what she wanted to accomplish and how it would align with her family life.

Once her vision was in place and she started taking action, our one-on-one sessions revealed her frustration around building the business to be operationally sound and moving into an ownership role. The frustration came from her strong value in the benefits of continuous learning and her partner's strong focus on continuous creating. The operation of the firm was misaligned because there was a lack of management skills in the daily operations and how they would lead together.

I proposed we do some partnership alignment exercises. We needed clarity about the firm's direction and how each partner would step forward to lead the effort. We also needed to identify gaps in skill set to build up their respective teams to run the daily operations. We employed two exercises on how to facilitate Team Value System and Organizational Value System. (I share these exercises later in this book for you to learn and leverage in your own environment.) The exercises resulted in clarity and a plan of action toward a joint vision they had never before expressed.

Their increased clarity on actions they could take together, the cadence of when they should focus on strategic goals, their effective articulations on how to meet with and build up their staff and how to best communicate the goals to their team to align strategy and move forward together—all of this changed their operational landscape to be more value driven. The two of them are creative and caring toward their team. They both employed my Leadership Circle 360 Profile assessment tool to rate the effectiveness of their leadership style in their environment. This gave us a map to best improve their skill set to increase their effectiveness.

What started as a coaching agreement with the CEO turned into a strategic growth and leadership advisory gig that makes me proud. In less than a year, these two leaders focused on the gaps in their skill set to build up a team that easily fills those gaps. They consistently focused on their strategic goals and increased communication to engage their staff so they would not feel alone in the charge. They empowered their team to rise to the occasion. They explored new tactics for sales and marketing to drive new business and enhance their reputation in the entertainment space. But I am most proud of their partnership growth. Their communication and ability to mark their gaps and to reach out for needed guidance is the best outcome I, as their coach and advisor, could have imagined. It means they know there will always be areas to enhance and that they are always in action toward their goals. Their attention to building up their team will move them from operating their business to owning it by Year Five.

Value Exchange Leadership™ works. The fact that you have this book in your hands means you want to level up your leadership style and might not be sure where to start. This book is your leverage. By offering these tools for leaders to strengthen their stance and help others grow around them, I extend my reach beyond what I can do as a single leader. The value I offer is to let you know you are not alone and that you have a community of other leaders on common ground who also desire to be value exchange leaders. You can all grow together.

My mission is to show you the value you have to offer, to help you connect and share it with others, and to see you receive value in return. What I know for sure is that, if I show leaders how to do this as well, the impact will be exponential. Leverage these tools and methods so you can build this type of exchange into your daily practice and grow as a leader. Most of all, pass it on so that others will gain, as well.

I designed a Value Exchange Leadership™ 90-Day Program for those who what to go deeper into the practice. This program gives you the guidance, support, and tools to break through to your leadership stance. As I said before, you are not alone in your journey, so please join me. At the back of the book is a special offer for when you apply for your spot in the elite coaching program. In the meantime, leverage the learning from this book and put the tools into practice. When you receive value from this, please share it with me across the social media or via email. That value-exchange confirmation means the world to me.

Are you ready to become a value exchange leader? Let's jump right in.

CHAPTER *Two*

"Daring leaders who live into their values are never silent about hard things."

BRENÉ BROWN, AUTHOR OF *DARE TO LEAD: BRAVE WORK. TOUGH CONVERSATIONS. WHOLE HEARTS.*

VALUE EXCHANGE LEADERSHIP™ DEFINED

Do you remember the first time you were asked to lead something? As I recall the first times I showed leadership qualities and capabilities, one common theme stands out in each interaction: I added value to every situation. Sometimes it was my ability to just Get Shit Done that people loved to lean on; other times it was my innate ability to listen, observe, and serve people's needs by communicating proposals how best to move forward. I learned I could delegate tasks and they would get done! It freed me up to do more, and that was a game changer for me that reshaped my leadership style. But my underlying desire to be of value and receive value from my career has always been the driving force to my decision process as I climbed the corporate ladder and became the CEO of my own business. The is how the methods of the value exchange leader came to fruition.

As I dove into sales and marketing concepts to build my business, I found value exchange to be prevalent in sales. Having studied and practiced it, I do that in every exchange I have. The rewards have impacted me not only monetarily, but in all arenas.

The value-based purchase concept is: When you purchase, you are receiving value in return for value. Marketing lessons abound on the perceived value to the customer for the price of the item that helps drive the purchasing decision. Commercials emote something that makes you want to buy. Regardless of your decision to purchase, you receive something for your hard-earned cash.

> *Value in marketing*, also known as **customer-perceived value**, is the difference between a prospective customer's evaluation of the benefits and costs of one product when compared with others.

Exceptional leadership entails multiple styles, methods, and qualifications. However, each environment, relationship, organizational structure, and growth plan influences your leadership effectiveness under each circumstance. In my executive leadership career, I have built teams, mentored leaders, and become a coach to help executive leaders navigate their path of effectiveness in the environments they have chosen or been appointed to. I've learned there's no one-size-fits-all method of leadership. There is, however, a common approach in a value exchange leader.

When you focus on value exchange in your leadership approach, you raise your fulfillment factor in all your interactions. You consistently understand that you have something of value to offer and something of value to gain. If you can master this mindset and put it into action with everything you do, your performance in all areas will increase. Most of all, you will build long-standing relationships with your employers, clients, teams, and peers.

What is VALUE EXCHANGE LEADERSHIP™?

Value Exchange Leadership™ is leading with clarity from your Personal Value System, understanding the values of the people you hire or work for, and consistently building value exchanges in every action.

We are all exposed to different forms of leadership and have responded in kind to being on the receiving end of stellar leaders and subpar leaders. It's confusing, right? Some leadership styles cause us to shine, while others make us recoil. One thing I know for sure: When you work for a firm that you do not own, you are working within a value system that dictates styles of leadership to deliver products and services to your client base. How was that value system created? It could have been established accidentally with no forethought due to market demands and limitations of the founding leaders; or it could have been meticulously curated by the founders to ensure their value system drives the company. Either way, you must decide (a) what is the best value system fit for you, and (b) how you will shine as a leader in this environment. So many factors shape our personal leadership style. If you picked up this book, you are willing to pursue a new way to lead and increase your effectiveness. I am excited to share my methods with you.

When I embarked on this process to combine all the best leadership lessons I had learned, I designed coaching programs to accompany this book. The combination helps individuals who feel stuck in their management level and don't have the guidance, support, and accountability to up-level in their careers. I have come across a lot of managers who got where they are by being competent in one area, who got promoted for that competency, and who desired to grow in title and income. But they were never taught how to identify the type of leader they really want to be. How you lead directly corresponds with what you value most and how you express that value to others.

Your Personal Value System

I define your Personal Value System as the combination of daily activities that bring you fulfillment and demonstrate to others what you value most. It's easy to fall into the trap of following other people's value systems in order to belong (tribal mentality);

we can feel lost when we try to identify this for ourselves. This book will help you identify what is true for you and increase your level of self-mastery in order to authentically lead those who follow. Holistic growth requires understanding your value system and articulating it to others.

We all wake up with an agenda, right? Even if it's not the ideal one just yet, you wake up with it. Your agenda nudges you to get out of bed in the morning. Most of us have habitual, must-accomplish tasks on our list, such as:

STANDARD AGENDA:

Wake up.
Turn off alarm.
Look at Instagram.
Scan emails (quick, before the kids wake up).
Throw on workout clothes.
Wake up kids.
Squeeze in a quick workout.
Make coffee.
Prepare breakfast for everyone.
Get everyone ready.
Check train schedule.
Watch the weather forecast.
Run through school drop-off.
Catch train.
Nap or check social media.
Grab a real coffee drink.
Reach your desk.
Start the work day.
Interact with the team.
Assess client needs.
Check in with the boss.
Sneak a lunch break (if you're lucky).
Return emails and calls.

Review train schedule and who's responsible for pick-up today.
Board train.
Catch up on news links and social media.
Arrive home and change clothes.
Cook and eat dinner with the family.
Tag team the kids' night routine.
Enjoy a nightcap while watching Netflix with spouse.
Fall into bed.
(Do it all again tomorrow.)

How you manage your time and the intention behind it is EVERYTHING! When you show up as a leader of your life *first*, it transcends into a value-based agenda in everything you do. Why? Because you are clear on where you are headed, and you maximize every second to create a high-value exchange to achieve the next rung of leadership.

Maybe you're thinking, "Kareen, you are being so abstract, I can't follow." No worries. Let me show you how leading with value shifts your daily agenda:

INTENTIONAL AGENDA:

Wake up.
Turn off alarm.
Do these things before your feet touch the ground:

- State three things you are grateful for and identify one win from yesterday.
- Set an intention for the day: "Today I will serve my team to my highest potential and help them grow in the best way I know how."

Hug and kiss the family and state what you hope for them today: "I love you and hope today you will learn something great about yourself."
Work out with thoughts of strength and resilience.
Make coffee.

Serve everyone breakfast.
Get everyone ready.
Check train schedule.
Watch the weather forecast.
Run through school drop-off.
Get to train.
Connect with one staff member or friend and let them know your appreciation for them and/or their work.
Grab real coffee drink for self and one to gift someone at work. (It's a giving game with your team to share gratitude, and today is your day.)
Drop stuff at your desk; gift co-worker their morning drink.
Start the day with a quick huddle of the team to understand each person's intention for the day, expressed in action statements. Ask, "How can I serve you today?"
Jump into action and fulfill your intention of the day.

- Assess client needs.
- Check in with the boss.

Have lunch with someone on the team in need of mentorship.
Return emails and calls.
Review train schedule and who's responsible for pick-up today.
Catch train.
Check email for daily intention follow-through email from the team to see who is crushing it and who is in need of assistance.
Return home and change clothes.
Engage in daily WELCOME HOME ritual with the whole family: high fives and hugs, state what you are grateful for today, and if there was a struggle, what help do you need to break through. (Everyone shares, even the youngest kids.)
Enjoy dinner with the family.
Tag team the kids' night routine.
Prepare routine for the next day's intention (fifteen minutes).

- Lay out workout clothes.
- List articles to read or podcasts to listen to on commute

to increase learning to share with team.

Download the day and motivation session with spouse/partner (Daily connection with a loved one is key for optimal performance inside and outside of the home. Check in with individual needs, family needs, individual wins for the day, and intention for the week.)

Sleep.

(Do it all again tomorrow.)

Do you see the difference? Do you feel the energy of showing up with intention versus showing up simply to check off an obligatory box? Which agenda propels your life forward? How would you feel if you put Agenda 2 into action? What values would you be displaying if you acted this way in everything you do?

If you read my first book, *Be A Badass: Six Tools to Up-Level Your Life*, you know that I was blindly focused on a career climb to create financial freedom. As I defined the VXL programs to assist executives to advance in their leadership style, I realized my style helped me maneuver my career, assist others to grow around me, and put me on a continuous growth path. I lead with value. Throughout my career, I have been recognized for my ability to motivate teams to deliver against obscene deadlines and for putting together complex products and services that satisfy our customers. I have leveraged this unique approach in my strategic consulting and coaching practice working with leaders one-on-one. My ability to see all parts of a whole, how others need to show up in it, and how to lead within these environments underlies an enhanced skill set.

I have always been open to learn more about myself and my needs through training programs and certification training, and I have done my best to put the information into practice for others to leverage. Now, after coaching and developing leaders for the last fifteen years and helping them develop these fundamental practices, I want to extend my reach and train more people in Value Exchange Leadership™.

VXL comes from leveraging your Personal Value System (PVS), building Team Value Systems (TVS), and integrating them into the Organizational Value System (OVS).

You commonly hear of a win-win or a win-lose situation. Worst case is a lose-lose scenario. Regardless of the outcome, it's considered a win or a loss because something of value was exchanged or taken. In a win-win, both parties have given and received value, and they walk away feeling fulfilled. It doesn't happen every time, but if you are a leader and you approach how you lead each interaction with value in mind (*How can I serve? How can I be of value?*), AND the person on the other side is asking the same questions of themselves, the end result will be a win-win. That is Value Exchange Leadership™.

When you are leading, you are never alone. You are a part of the whole. Focus on a value exchange for everyone involved in your system, and you will excel in your leadership role.

CHAPTER *Three*

"Leadership is not about titles,

positions or flow charts.

It is about one life influencing another."

JOHN C. MAXWELL, CEO AND FOUNDER THE JOHN MAXWELL COMPANY

WHAT DOES LEADERSHIP MEAN TO YOU?

Did you become a leader from desire or by default? Today's corporate environment is comprised of a vastly growing digital landscape. Millennials entering the workforce are demanding more than menial, task-completion jobs. To dedicate their time to a firm, they want to be seen and to feel useful. The old ways of annual performance appraisals and potential promotion have become unsustainable. When you marry a desire for meaningful work that has growth potential (the milennial desire), with a previous workforce that received inflated payrolls for unrefined skillsets, handed out without earning the income received by massive growing tech companies, the demands to be an effective leader becomes challenging. There are many different dynamics to navigate. The days of just having a strong work ethic, a willingness to learn, and a qualified skillset are swept under the rug for personality management, team building, and how many ways you can materially give to your employees to get them to do something with passion versus apathy. Facing all that, along with other long standing dynamics regarding diversity and equal pay hiring practices, leading in today's market can be overwhelming. Knowing why you want to lead is critical for effectiveness in today's work environments. Learning ways to lead and ensuring that those you work with understand your values and that you also respect their values quiets the noise and allows you to step forward into action with ease.

Let's dig into why you chose to lead. What drove you up the ladder for a leadership position? How important is the title, the role and responsibility, and the impact you will have as a leader? Some people achieve a management position by default there is simply no one else willing or available to take on the responsibility. Some people attain a management position because "that's the way to advance at the firm and make more money"—more responsibility equals higher pay. But is that where you really want to be? I have seen time and again layers of managers, people with high-level titles and no true leadership skills, get away with mistreating their staff. I have seen top performers leave the firm in frustration because they are skilled but are not being heard. When individuals are awarded a title to lead, but they have no desire to lead, it stunts the growth of their team and the business. It creates high levels of attrition and cross-department mishap that affects operational efficiency and loss of market share simply from condoning the inability to lead. Becoming more self-aware of how you show up and get clear on what you value most can shift this dynamic.

What Track Are You On

Leaders need to know where they are headed, so they can lead others in that direction as well. I ask senior executives who are unsure about the direction they want to go, "If you were a C-Suite leader, which leadership role would you be excited to step into?" This helps identify what skill set is required to qualify for the position. It also helps build a leadership growth plan that aligns with your Personal Value System.

C-SUITE BREAKDOWN

Most people don't really pay attention to the C-Suite roles and responsibilities until it is something in their purview of growth, or they decide to launch their own business and step into a C-Suite role by default, not yet having the experience. As you work on your exercise to envision the leadership role you want to play, know that titles are great, but they come with significant responsibility, and they require a skill set to succeed. When you understand what is best for your value system and climb into one of these roles, you can envision how it will fit the value system of the organization you plan to lead. Here is a quick overview to help you understand the specifics of each C-Suite role. As you review my personal definition and skills per role, keep in mind that the actual job description for any company would outline the true level of responsibility and ownership within the firm. These descriptions will show you the common traits of someone in each role, so you can decide what track you desire. Selecting a track as a North Star for your leadership path helps you assess what you have already, and it helps us craft the action plan to help you achieve it.

Here is how I define the key traits for the role and responsibility of each C-Suite member:

CEO-Chief Executive Officer.

Master and pied piper of the business. Consistently steers the company for growth in sales, acquires top leaders to outperform competitors, sets the tone for the Organizational Value System, empowers the C-Suite leaders to fulfill their responsibilities, facilitates strategic decisions among the Board of Directors, listens to client demand, and builds the infrastructure of the organization. Generally, has equity stake in the business performance and is responsible for sales, strategic growth decisions, and partnerships. Represents the brand ethos, the sustainability of the business, and the overall financial health of the company.

*Requires masterful ability to direct and steer the company for growth. A relational person who seeks ways to expand offerings and build business with others.

CFO-Chief Financial Officer.

Manages the money. Sometimes responsible for accounting, payroll, vendor management, legal, and human resources. Works with the CEO and the COO on forecasts of future projections for the firm based on sales and operational optimization. Always focuses on the impact to the bottom line and strategies of risk mitigation.

*Requires mastery in risk mitigation, sourcing funds, and accounting practices to sustain the growth of the business in fluctuating markets.

CTO-Chief Technology Officer.

Manages the technical offering of the firm to external clients. Responsible for in-house development teams. Dictates methods of technical delivery, compliance, stability, and performance of technical products to the customer. Works directly with the CEO to ensure the products delivered meet market demand against the strategy of the business.

*Requires mastery in staying abreast of the latest technical offerings and keeping the company up-to-date or ahead of time with their product suite to stay relevant in the industry.

CIO-Chief Information Officer.

Responsible for traditional information technology and computer systems that support enterprise goals. May also include data management and analytics to ensure the infrastructure is aligned to report on data flow of the business. Provides reports to help the business make decisions on where to pivot their offering. Can report in this service role to multiple C-Suite leaders to ensure their department needs are met.

*Requires mastery in information security, technical infra-structure, process, and operations to sustain a compliant technical stack to run the business demands and service internal team needs.

CPO-Chief Product Officer.

Sometimes known as Chief Innovation Officer. Corporate title refers to an executive responsible for various product-related activities in an organization. The ideas person who marries client demand with product creation. Most often the position reports to the CEO.

*Requires mastery to stay on top of trends in the market, has an ear to the ground with the client base, is an innovative, solution-driven thinker, and has a keen design skill set.

CMO-Chief Marketing Officer.

Leads brand management, marketing communications (including advertising, promotions, and public relations), market research, sales management, product development, distribution channel management, pricing, and customer service.

*Requires mastery in creating the user experience across the product and business brand that sustains returning customers and attracts new buyers across all product offerings.

CRO-Chief Revenue Officer.

Responsible for all revenue-generation processes in an organization. Accountable for driving better integration and alignment between all revenue-related functions, including marketing, sales, customer support, pricing, and revenue management.

*Requires mastery in strategic thinking and execution to build new revenue streams once existing strategies have been maximized. Has expertise in marketing and sales tactics to drive execution plans.

COO-Chief Operating Officer.
Responsible for the daily operation of the company.

*Requires mastery in aligning people, processes, and technology to deliver optimized operations and sustain a lean operating expense and maximum profits. Sees all, hears all, pivots and tweaks operations with ease. Thrives when change is demanded to realign new operational tactics to meet new demands.

Now that you understand the highest leadership roles in a firm, what speaks to you? What track do you see yourself on, if any? If you can't identify with any of these, write down why. It is 100 percent okay to face the reality that corporate climbing is not for you. However, if it is out of fear for not knowing how to achieve it, then write down that missing piece so we can solve for it. Remember, this book is a guide to lead with a value exchange in mind, and if you don't believe these roles align with your value vision path, then you can design a role that works for you.

Are You an Owner or an Operator?
Some of you may be owners of your business and play all the C-Suite roles, because you are currently in the startup to grow-up phase. In my opinion, the way you lead this phase matters most to the trajectory of your business. As an equity stake owner in your business, you must decide if you are an operator or an owner. They are two different leadership stances and require understanding to help you chart your leadership vision.

I worked with a CEO of a startup in the second year of business, focusing on her leadership vision and the company role she wanted to play. Time and again, when startup CEOs build their business, they are quickly bogged down with tasks and activities that they do because they *can*. They don't stop to think about *why* they are doing it or whether it is the best use of their time. If you don't focus on why you are leading, what you really want to be doing, where you want to grow, and whom you want to impact, your capacity to grow the business gets stunted. I asked her, point-blank, "Do you envision being the long-term OPERATOR of your business, or do you want to OWN your business?"

Operators need to run the daily activities of the business. Owners have built the systems and operations and hired the appropriate team of leaders to run their business, so they can earn the income from the concept and move on to the next ownership venture. Even as a full-time employee of firms, I would do my best to play an owner role. I did that by ensuring others would step in to replace me so that I could step into the leadership role of owning the function.

A light bulb went on for this CEO when we completed her vision exercise. She saw a three-year plan to establish long-standing, scalable operations, during which she would be the acting CEO to build the business and income she knew it offered. But underneath, she saw herself owning this business, so she could build another stream of income through her speaking engagements and coaching practice to help other businesses do the same.

It was a remarkable moment of excitement and relief to help her define what was most important to her now and define an outcome of impact she could lean into with enthusiasm. We could now map out a strategic action plan for the next three, six, nine, and twelve months. The plan was to build the foundation that would let her step away 50 percent of the time to work toward the two-year goal of being away 75 percent of the time. Next, she could step into 100 percent ownership with only 1 percent effort of leadership.

Imagine having a strategy like this for your personal leadership growth! The concept applies equally to internal executives and

C-Suite leaders of start-up environments. All you need are the tools to apply it to you.

At times, leaders all question where we are headed next. If you don't focus on what is next, you, your team, and your business will not grow. You can break useless patterns and create new ones that drive you forward into a more fulfilled life as a leader. You are 100 percent in control of the life you lead and how you lead it. You just need the tools and action plan to achieve it.

EXERCISE:

Your Leadership Vision

It's easy to put your career on autopilot. That may be fine for most, but if you want to lead and advance in your career, autopilot does not work. To be clear, autopilot means you plan for yourself, your business, and your team ONLY once a year. You map out the vision, you are excited for about a week, and then you jump back into old habits. Time passes until you hit that annual mark and realize what you chartered toward last year did not happen. You scrap it and build a new plan that again goes stale in a week or two.

Stop the cycle! Bring in new methods to clarify your vision and practice daily to achieve it.

To move toward your desired career, you need to identify your North Star. Right here, right now, we will take the first few steps and put it on paper, so you can easily work toward your vision.

STEP 1—TAKE INVENTORY

Write down an inventory of your skills, qualifications, and activities across the career roles you have played that you are **most proud of**. Consider the roles you have played in life and in business and list all the different skills and qualifications you have gained over time. Use as many pages as it takes. You can refer to your résumé too, but that may not list your actual skills. Elaborate on it. Include extracurricular items such as sports, cooking, travel, arts, whatever you do that represents a skill.

Title: _____

Company: _____

Skills/Qualifications/Activities:

- • _____
- • _____

Title: _____

Company: _____

Skills/Qualifications/Activities:

- • _____
- • _____

Shooooot, you have skills! Look at the value you bring to the table!

STEP 2—FULFILLMENT FACTOR

Go back through the list and score each item on a scale of one to ten (one being no fulfillment, ten being so fulfilled you want to burst). Your degree of fulfillment for each task will help you assess if you want to use these skills in the future or simply leverage them to get to the next level of your career.

STEP 3—GROUPING

On a separate sheet of paper, list everything that ranks eight and above.

STEP 4—DREAM BIG!

Grab another sheet of paper.

Now that you are gleaming with pride, take a minute and **consider the ideal life role you would like to play**. Think five, ten, twenty years from now. Don't limit yourself based on your current situation—focus on what you dream of becoming. Who is that?

When you cast a career-based vision of who you want to be, do it with super clarity: Use descriptive adjectives for what you do, who you lead, the impact you make in your company, community, and the world. What does your workspace look like? Who are your clients? What is your bank balance? What are the biweekly check amounts, the annual amounts, and bonuses for doing this amazing work? What do people call you? What is your role/title? Be creative and dream big. What is your vision?

Write it down:

- _____
- _____
- _____
- _____
- _____
- _____

Here's the deal: If you are unclear on where you are headed, then you can't map a path to get there. Sometimes, dreaming big and casting a vision feels hard because we are used to focusing on what is not working. We are so bogged down by the daily grind that our dream is numb. Step number one to shift your career is to know where you want to go. If you cannot visualize how your career impacts your life and creates the lifestyle you dream of, then there is a disconnect in your actions today. To build a fulfilled life, find alignment between what you love and what you do to create the income to afford what you love. A value exchange can happen with no monetary gain and give you highly fulfilled moments—but imagine being handsomely paid for the value you bring to the table every single day! That's the importance of a clear vision of leading your life and your teams. Without a North Star, you have no compass. If you struggle with mapping this out on your own, join my Value Exchange Leadership™ 90-Day Mastermind, and get the clarity you seek.

Look back at what you have written. If it's vague, like _I want to be CEO of the company I work for_, that is a title goal, not a career goal. Explain _why_ you want that role and be explicit as to what that role means to you.

Now that you have written out your vision, make a concrete vision board that displays your dream. A vision board that you see every day creates a constant, impactful reminder that crystalizes the vision into reality. To create your vision board, consider:

What does your office look like? Who are you leading? Where are your clients? How do you run meetings with them (over fancy dinners or lunches, on the golf course, over a home-cooked meal)? What is your truth in your vision of doing business and acting as a leader? What kind of car do you drive? What do you wear? What charities do you run or contribute to? What does this role provide your family? Do you take vacations? Do your kids attend private school? Start with the career life in the middle and expand the imagery of how this career life integrates into your personal life.

Grab some images off the internet and put a visual board together of the life you desire to lead.

If you are unsure of what is possible, dream something up (write your own script!) or think about someone whose lifestyle and career you want to emulate. This will clarify your likes and dislikes to create the role you love.

Clarity on Your Role

I mapped out each major promotion in my career based on my vision. I took the time to ask myself, "What next?" I wrote the description of my next desired role, the culture of the company, the type of people I wanted to work with, whom I wanted working for me, whom I wanted to impact, what I wanted to learn from each role, what I wanted to take away. My clarity made my search easy because I focused on what I wanted and made clear what didn't fit, so I could move past it. I also assessed the skills I needed to step into the role. I made sure that each opportunity I said *yes* to helped me gain that additional skill set. Do you see how much easier getting into action will be if you can identify where you are headed?

This works well in a corporate environment because your managers generally **do not** have a growth path for you unless they, themselves, are growing. You can easily present to them what you really want and know what is possible in your current firm when you are clear on what you want versus waiting for them to suggest it. And if the answer is, "No, that opportunity is not possible here," then you will know sooner that the company you are working for is not a fit. You can work on your exit strategy to find the company that matches what you want. If you are not advancing yourself first, you will never learn how to advance anyone who reports to you. Then you are all stuck. Your choice.

I chose to lead by example. When I first started my career, I was a very controlling, process-oriented, get-shit-done kind of woman. I took the bull by the horns and steered it my way. It was effective in most of my roles, and it helped me navigate into senior leadership roles because I filled the gaps by doing work that others did not want to do. I did the work myself, then I trained someone to replace me, so I could move on to other challenges and grow in my role. With each growth spurt, I asked for a pay raise or compensation for the larger task at hand. A lot of us fear asking for something in return for doing more, and that perpetuates an imbalanced value cycle. When we do not receive fair value in return for our hard work, we feel victimized and disempowered.

Monetary gain is not the only way to compensate hard work. Money is a driving force to make hard work worthwhile, so you can afford more luxuries in your home life or spend the extra earnings on a much-needed vacation, but that only goes so far to fulfill our human needs. Understanding what drives you is key to navigating how you show up and what you choose to accept. I call this your *Personal Value System.*

CHAPTER *Four*

"The truth is that, no matter where you started out in life, you have a choice between scarcity and abundance."

LISA NICHOLS, AUTHOR OF *AMPLIFY YOUR LIFE & ACHIEVE PROSPERITY TODAY*

FORMING YOUR PERSONAL VALUE SYSTEM

What was your first job and why did you get it? You were probably a teenager and needed some extra cash. You found a skill level position that you could do: a waitress, a summer camp counselor, a babysitter, a retail salesperson, an office mailroom clerk, and a house cleaner or a handyperson or a yard worker for your parents, etc. In that scenario, you still were not clear on your skill-set offering, your leadership style, or your capabilities because you were at the very beginning of your career journey. However, by saying *yes* to the job offered to you, an exchange took place. You added value to whomever you were working for by doing a job they needed, and they paid you for it. Score!

As your skills evolved, you probably received a higher level of education and exposure to new thought, new fields of business, and new career paths. Your career vision was forming. What did you look for when you chose your path? Was it some combination of growing your skill set, earning a certain income, and having the opportunity to grow within the organization once you got the job? You may not have been super clear on how to achieve it, but you saw something or someone in a role that you wanted to emulate or experience. Or maybe you were told you were good at something, so you should go after it. You applied for positions that might be good for you, and you prepared a résumé to explain your qualifications and experience. What were your criteria for the job hunt? If the job was offered to you, what did you consider about the company and the role and responsibility of the job?

Sometimes when we move forward under someone else's plan for us, we forget to ask ourselves: *Is this what I really want? Is this enough?* I learned to keep my eyes open to see where I was adding value and to assess if I could grow in return. Growth is one of my guiding principles. Here's the best lesson I learned in my twenties that helped me shape my career-path decisions:

In my twenties, it was about survival. It was about earning an income. I was willing to try any job in a reputable company with growth potential to pay my bills and not feel strapped. I was willing to exchange whatever value I bring to the table for money and some stability. That was my value exchange focus at the time. Sound familiar?

At the ripe young age of twenty-three, I hit a glass ceiling. I had been on the job for about eight months. My new manager was fierce. I was excited to have someone with experience to teach me how to build my career and grow within my role. However, this woman had a different agenda. What I did not realize was that she felt threatened by me.

My support team members habitually came to me for advice, process layout, and task distribution. Every time my manager asked other team members what they do and how they do it, all roads led back to me as the "manager" of it all. I was only doing what I thought best for the team and our internal clients. I was front-line support, so I received all the requests and distributed them. I also was responsible for business resumption if system errors occurred to stop daily operations, and I was the catalyst for the team to resolve the issues. It was way more than I was hired to do, but it needed to be done.

Eventually, I needed to know what direction it was headed. I had scheduled a one-on-one with my new boss to help her understand my role on the team and to ask for guidance about what was next. I put together a two-column list: On the left were requirements of the job I had been hired for eight months ago, and on the right was a list of the actual tasks I now focused on. I wanted to illustrate the increase in duties and responsibilities so that she would have full knowledge of my contributions and could help me see how to grow with this team. We were in a four-person conference room, and I prepared myself for the meeting by taking deep breaths and saying to myself, "Kareen, you have nothing to lose. Tell her where you are, and I am sure she will guide you with next steps."

We started the meeting, and I realized she never smiled when she looked at me. I think the Army had trained her for intimidation tactics twenty years prior. I began by thanking her for meeting with me to discuss my current role and to help me understand how I could grow on the team. I showed her my document and walked her through my activities. Then I asked what she thought and if she saw a growth plan for me.

I will never forget her reaction. With a smirk on her face she said, "Kareen, I don't know what you are complaining about. What you are doing is your job. Just keep doing it." Then she ended the meeting, and that was that. No mention of how long I would need to do this job to grow into something else, no thoughts or consideration on how to increase my skill set so I could earn more and grow within the company. Nothing.

I felt deflated. Why was I doing so much? Why was I stretching so much for a job and a manager who would not help me get to the next level? I was overwhelmed with emotion. I was thankful it was a Thursday, so I would only have to show up on Friday and then have the weekend to decide what to do next. I was in shock. Over the weekend, I assessed the pros and cons of staying in the job. I felt paralyzed. I couldn't believe it was really true. Once reality set in, I knew what I had to do. On Monday morning, I sent my resignation email to my boss. I gave her two weeks, and I was out.

As scary as it was, I knew I had made the right decision when the firm replaced me with a man and paid him $22,000 more than what they had paid me. My replacement got to hire an assistant at $45,000 to do all the work that I had done for the team! All I had asked for was a growth plan and ability to earn more. I was making $38,000 at the time and had been replaced by two men for a cost to the company of $105,000. This was the best lesson for me so early in my career because it taught me three things:

> #1—*People lead through their own limitations, and their limitations are not for me to carry, nor do they represent my capacity or my worthiness.*

> #2—*Always ask for what you think you deserve. If the answer is no, then it is your choice to embrace the no and decide what is right for you.*

> #3—*Taking a risk to go after what you want is more fulfilling than facing a dead end with no growth opportunity.*

In that position, I had been leading without benefit of the title. I led without recognition, and I led without guidance from my managers. My team loved working with me, my clients appreciated my efforts, and they relied on me 24/7. But I felt I was delivering a higher value than I received. I was stuck in the I'm-so-lucky-to-have-this-job mentality. As a result, my health suffered, my relationships failed, and I felt like crap every day because the exchange was uneven. When I outlined my worth to my manager, I hit the glass ceiling. I had outgrown the current system, and I knew I could find another that would have a higher value exchange for me. I did not fail the system; the system failed me.

When I left that company, my value structure was different from when I first started because my value proposition was higher. I now had more skills, experience, know-how, abilities, and qualifications. I could level up my search and find something with greater responsibility and growth because I had proved I was capable. I also realized that sacrificing my Personal Value System for a check was not sustainable for a thriving life. These elements shape my ability to lead others. I never wanted anyone who I worked with to feel undervalued. In order to avoid that, I needed to understand their Personal Value System, so we could find a mutually beneficial exchange. But first, I had to find a leader and company that aligned with my value system.

I was fortunate to go to work for an amazing leader who was part of an outstanding corporate value system. That position helped me shape my leadership style, flex my muscles, and grow rapidly as I navigated in under five years from an individual contributor to a Senior Tech Manager for more than thirty-five people. I leveraged my skill set, my communication skills, my adaptability to different environments, and my capacity to plow through stress. I focused on creating a value-driven role in the company, where the CTO and CEO both recognized me as an asset to the company and continued to create new opportunities for me to sustain the growth I sought. I eventually outgrew some parts of the system and shifted my personal goals; then I exited graciously and with ease, knowing it was time for something else.

Let's focus on the moments in leading that shaped my value system at that firm. Before I joined the company, I questioned whether I should take the offer because the salary was lower than what I had earned in my previous job. It was a three-thousand-dollar difference—at that time a lot to consider, since every penny counts when you are living hand-to-mouth. However, the value exchange on the part of the company to allow me to grow, learn, and enhance my skill set ranked higher on my value exchange scale than pay. The fact that the company had a female CEO and CTO was a big win for me because I wanted to be a part of a company that valued female leaders. I did not want to repeat the experience from my last firm, where the two female managers I worked for did not value growth as I did. Also, the hiring manager for this position had a totally different skill set from mine. I knew if I said yes to this position, I would learn a side of the business I had never been exposed to before, and he would be able to lean on me for the skills I brought to the table. I appreciated the value exchange that would occur just by working for him. Since my value exchange score was high for this opportunity, I said *yes*. Even though the pay was lower, given the opportunity to grow, it would not be lower for long. I was confident of the value I offered.

Twenty years later, I still have a healthy relationship with that hiring manager, and we still add value to each other's lives. We have not worked together for eighteen years. He was my direct manager for about a year and a half, but his leadership style, focus on the agenda at hand, communication tactics, sales tactics, and team building helped shape my leadership career path.

When you expose yourself to effective leadership styles and start to design your own, it shapes what arenas you can work within. My five years with that company were not easy. I had to earn my place. I don't have a magic pill that will solve all your career challenges, but I can help you discover what is most important for you to focus on and experience every single day. And I can help you recognize where you are willing to compromise because it doesn't keep you from advancing, from getting promoted to the next level, or from completing that next step to achieve your goals. Also, it helps shape the legacy you will leave behind. Maintaining a relationship for twenty years where we both know we can call for assistance and the other will show up—that is the ultimate value exchange.

The Personal Value System (PVS) shapes how I assess opportunities, and it helps my clients develop personal strategies to align their values with the values of the companies they work for. It also helps them recognize if their career is stunted due to an outdated value exchange model. Either way, identifying the value proposition and exchange between you and the system you want to grow within is the key to navigating into the role you truly desire.

The next chapter will help illuminate your current value proposition and then clarify your ultimate role as a thriving leader. I will offer some tools and methods to assess the effectiveness of your leadership style in your current system. And most of all, you will identify what the ultimate value exchange is to you, so you know what actions to take next.

Think about your Personal Value System versus that of the company you wish to work for or the one that you build for yourself and those you employ. Personal values lead your decisions. When you are disgruntled at your job, it is not because of the actual work you are doing; it's more likely about how you are being treated, spoken to, and ultimately valued by your firm. Most people choose to leave their job when they stop growing in their position and it becomes monotonous, or because they don't get along with a leader or manager they work with. The growth part is easy to fix; opportunities abound for a more challenging job in a challenging environment. If you have the skills, you can snatch up that opportunity. But the personality conflicts and inability to communicate properly create an underlying value system in your corporate culture, and it weighs against your Personal Value System. When these two systems don't line up, a different kind of search is needed to decide if this company is right for you or if it is time to move on.

▶ CHAPTER *Five*

"Take the opportunity to learn from your mistakes: find the cause of your problem and eliminate it. Don't try to be perfect; just be an excellent example of being human."

TONY ROBBINS, FOUNDER AND CEO OF ANTHONY ROBBINS RESEARCH

YOUR CORE VALUES DRIVE ALL OF YOUR ACTIONS

Before you can judge whether a company's value system is right for you, you need to understand your own value system. What is important for you to thrive? If your values are unclear, then the companies you say *yes* to may never be a fit. It is completely okay at the start of your career to say *yes* to companies and test what works, because you don't yet know what you are looking for. But your Personal Value System is all yours. It comes from how you choose to interact with others and show them how they should treat you in order to be in your life. We tend to swallow a lot in our workplace in order to find our way and earn income. That may be warranted when you are not the owner or C-Suite leader of the firm who sets the tone for running the company. And if you are the C-Suite leader but the company performance doesn't align with your expectations or demands, there is probably a misalignment of value systems across your organization. You must know what you value most in a work environment for you to operate at your best and grow; otherwise, you will be stunted and start looking for something else faster than it took to sign that offer letter.

Let's identify what you value most, so you can easily articulate it to others. I recently had a one-on-one session with a CFO I have been coaching for over two years. I was excited to hear how she shared her values with the founders of the business she works for, the CEO and COO (who happened to be married and brought a lot of dysfunction into the workplace). Up until this point, my client, the CFO, had carried the burden of lifting morale in her group and tried to fix problems that were not aligned with her value system. She tried to create an acceptable environment, but in reality, it totally compromised her value system. She hired me, so she could break the cycle of cleaning up everyone else's mess and step firmly into her leadership role. She wanted to initiate and lead environments with a strong value exchange, so everyone wins. What better test to get clarity on your values than working through a dysfunctional environment and still finding success in the work that you do?

She recounted her stance in a conversation with the CEO about an unacceptable action by an employee (who happened to be the son of the owners). She felt this employee acted outside of the standards that the leadership team held for everyone else. My client decided that, this time, she would not let it slide. From this point forward, the passive behavior of the CEO and COO around such incidents would no longer be tolerated. She was clear, and she stated her truth—it made me proud! Our work over the last two years had brought her to this point. She used to suffer in silence and carry the burden of the dysfunctional leadership style of her counterparts. She tried to make up for the volatile environ-ment they created by having meetings behind closed doors to smooth things over. She would constantly clean up the mess, and as much as there is reward in being the hero, she was broken down, tired, and disconnected from her values—integrity, truth, and inspiration. She now sees the importance of standing in her truth. She has realized that in order to lead with these values front and center, she must dismiss the moments that don't align with her role and responsibility. She must not enable the bad behavior, and she must call it out when lines are crossed.

Through certification programs with top mindset coach Tony Robbins and top empathy coach Brené Brown, I have learned different ways to identify what I value most, and I have shared the extensive training exercises with my clients and in my hands-on training and development program. To help you determine your value set, I will share a simple exercise with you here.

In my training to become a Certified Holistic Health Coach from the Institute of Integrative Nutrition, I learned to use Maslow's hierarchy of needs to study how humans intrinsically partake in behavioral motivation. Maslow used the terms "physiological," "safety," "belonging and love," "esteem," and "self-actualization" to describe the pattern through which human motivations generally move. For motivation to occur at the next level, each prior level must be satisfied within the individual. Furthermore, this theory is a key to understanding how drive and motivation are correlated in relation to human behavior. Each of these individual levels contains a certain amount of internal sensation that must be met for an individual to complete their hierarchy. The goal of Maslow's theory is to attain the fifth level or stage: self-actualization. I share this with you because we all suffer and thrive based on our human needs. When we grow more comfortable communicating our needs and our values,we become more self-aware and better able to connect with others.

At Tony Robbins's Unleash the Power Within seminar, I learned his breakdown of the six human needs that somewhat relates to Maslow's levels. Tony stated we have four primary needs (certainty, variety, significance, and love/connection) and two spiritual needs (growth and contribution). These four guiding forces drive how we behave and how we show up to meet a need. Self-awareness of where we focus most leads us to a desire for growth and impact—which are strong driving forces when we want something new and seek ways to lead others and share our learning. Tony also says our

Primary Question filters our conscious and unconscious thinking on a consistent basis. Our Primary Question becomes the ultimate laser for what we consistently notice or fail to notice and experience in our lives.

My Primary Question came to me in a whisper and surprised me. At the start of my work with Tony Robbins, my Primary Question was: "Am I good enough?" So many of my behaviors, thoughts, and actions were either to prove I was good enough or tear myself down because I believed I was not good enough. The benefit of this laser focus on my Primary Question is that it revealed overachievement in multiple arenas where I pushed harder to prove I was enough. It then would fail me as a focus because I always believed that, no matter how much I tried, I was never enough. From a young age, I was subjected to a comparison-based society and critical feedback. It tore me down and made me feel small. It instilled my belief that I was not worthy, that I was not enough, and that I would never be enough. As you can imagine, it held me back from living out my true values, because I did not think I was worthy of living the life I desired. I didn't know what worthiness felt like.

Achievement was my source of escapism and gave me the freedom to invest in a new story and build a new Primary Question over time. It made me more in tune with myself and drove me forward in alignment with my Personal Value System. My top three values are: Trust, Integrity, and Truth. When I think about being "enough", it is in comparison to someone else's definition of enough, not my own. Having this Primary Question as my guiding force explained so much about my life experience. I was successful in business because I could achieve and manage very complex situations and dismiss my own needs in order to impress others in exchange for title and income. It fulfilled my human need for significance. I have a strong sense of certainty in my capabilities and what I can accomplish because I had proven I could push through anything to achieve "success" when I set my mind to it. I also thrived in variety because when things were not enough or there was a level of disappointment in how I show up, I could easily switch my focus to a new project, move to another city, or start over. Really, all I wanted to feel was love and connection, to be accepted for who I am and how I show up, without comparison. I wanted to be enough.

This realization helped me achieve my desire without posturing anymore. My clients use this technique to articulate their needs. That enables them to show up clearly with their teams and their clients. They easily define their Primary Question, and it guides them as they navigate reactions to the Primary Question.

My current Primary Question is: "How can I appreciate, receive, give, and enjoy the love in my life with every action I take?" It might sound corny, but sit with it. Imagine, as a leader, acknowledging the truth of what you really want to feel and be every day. Imagine if you could simplify your guiding principles to be actionable and to feel it in the moment! How fulfilling would your day be? My shift— from *am I enough* to *how can I appreciate, receive, give, and enjoy the love in my life*—has been a complete game changer. It evokes value exchange with every step I take. When you know the guiding force of basic human needs, you can better articulate why you show up this way, and it also helps you see how others show up for you.

Your current Primary Question (and the human need it meets) reveals what drives you forward and what shuts you down or makes you pull away. As a leader, focusing on growth and impact/ contribution becomes natural once you achieve a higher level of self-awareness. You reap the benefits of doing the work both to articulate your needs and to understand the needs of others. If you want an immersion program where you can do the work on yourself and come out with an action plan to realize your truth, I highly recommend Tony Robbins's seminar, Unleash the Power Within. And if you are in a relationship, bring your partner. You will not want to build this new skill set without your significant other understanding it, too.

Trust me, you will make some amazing connections through these programs. If you want to do personal work of less intensity, check out my Be A Badass: Six Tools to Up-Level Your Life Book and Online Program. It's a jump-start with tools and actions to leverage for self-mastery. It builds a strong foundational skill set, especially as we do deeper work together in your leadership stance.

Dismissing the Debauchery

It takes time and effort to define your Personal Value System and learn how to lean easily into it. The practical knowledge from this book can put you into immediate action. I am going to share an exercise to increase the value of your time and define your core values, so you can create the framework.

Have you ever wanted to stop time, so you can cozy up and appreciate the life you have? Unfortunately, we cannot control the passage of time, but the cool thing is, we can control what we do with our time. We all have twenty-four hours in a day. The difference between someone who feels that time passes too quickly and someone who doesn't even notice time passing is how they choose to spend it.

We all have obligations that we dread. We all have moments of overwhelm trying to do it all. What we focus on and how it fills us up affects how we feel as time passes. When time is filled less with regret and more with empowered thinking, the return on investment for time spent increases. This exercise will help you align who you really are with what you do, and it will help you dismiss the debauchery of distraction that keeps you from living a highly valued life.

To raise our level of fulfillment, we need to lean into our values and let go of distractions. Letting go is one of the hardest things to learn and master. If the concept makes you uncomfortable, you are not alone. But the tips you are about to receive will change the game of how you decide to spend your time. Stick with me.

As we evolve into the next version of ourselves, it is hard to let go of behaviors that no longer serve us and instead lean into the values that help us thrive. It's critical to align our Personal Value System with that of the ecosystem within which we work and live. If my clients feel discomfort in this, we trace it back to misalignment with the PVS, and we create an action to reframe perspective. They can then decide what the next action will be: What will realign the situation? Is it time to look at walking away, ending the relationship, resigning from the position?

Moments of upset, frustration, or obsession over an unresolved incident stem from a misalignment or challenge to core values. That truth can be difficult to stand in, but it is the fastest way to know what to do next and to jump into it.

I would love to help you move forward through pain and discomfort to find fulfillment. I get excited when I know I am going to end something, shut it down, and move on! Does that sound insane? Even though my heart is racing as I plan how to execute an ending and I am completely unsure how the decision will be received, I know that being on the other side of the decision means I am being true to myself. That excites me to my core!

What pushes me to the edge and makes me jump into uncertainty is to imagine how it will feel when the dysfunction ends. Knowing I will no longer force myself to show up in an environment that brings me down helps me muster up the courage to act. I love that moment right before I jump off the edge, not knowing how it will land with others, leaning into my self-certainty that standing in my truth will make me free. IT IS SO WORTH IT!

When I first prioritized my values over the perception of others, the good feeling was addictive. Standing my ground, speaking my truth, and making life-altering decisions was not easy. For years, I was miserable inside from sticking with situations, relationships, jobs, and a lifestyle that did not align with who I really am. Dismissing the debauchery and focusing on what fills me up has led me here, where I help others do the same. Without that learning, I would not have realized my super powers and built a business that I enjoy running every day. I would not have the strong relationships that lift me up and challenge me to be my best. When you flex this muscle in your mindset, you will be stronger in everything you do.

 EXERCISE:
Core Value Identity and Protection

STEP 1—IDENTIFY VALUES
Ask yourself, "What are the top three values that shape my Personal Value System?" For a list of potential values, visit www.kareenwalsh. com/valuesexercise. Write each of your value words on an individual sticky note.

STEP 2—RECORD AN INCIDENT
Ask yourself, "What is the incident I struggle with? Write it down on another sticky note.

STEP 3—IDENTIFY THE CHALLENGE
Ask yourself, "Based on this incident, which personal value is being challenged the most?" Attach that value sticky note to the note of the incident you are struggling with.

STEP 4–IDENTIFY THE POSSIBILITIES
Ask yourself, "If I were to stand in this value and be true to myself, what would I do different to manage this situation?" You can have multiple answers here; write them all down.

STEP 5–ACTION STEP
Ask yourself, "What can I do right now to alleviate the distraction I feel from this incident and realign with my core values?" Again, you may have multiple answers; write them all down.

With this exercise you have identified your core values, you have revisited an incident that does not serve you or that causes you stress, and you have devised a game plan to raise the vibration in your core values, to lean into who you really are, and to align your time with what is most valuable to you. WHAT A GIFT!

CHAPTER Six

"The responsibility of leadership is not to come up with all the ideas. The responsibility of leadership is to create an environment in which great ideas can thrive."

SIMON SINEK

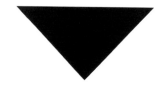

HOW TO CREATE YOUR TEAM VALUE SYSTEM

Your duty as team leader is to set the tone, but your team has the right to dictate their collective value system. How much of your leadership style is dictator-to-subordinate? When you call all the shots on how others should behave and deliver, you take 100 percent responsibility for everything and reduce the team's power to less than 1 percent. How can they do their job? Some environments warrant this style of leadership to keep everyone safe. Think about the military and the guidance that comes from a commander to his soldiers. A commander who does not dictate and a soldier who does not comply put the whole group at risk for injury or even death. For a commander to grow in his role, he must identify who among the ranks can balance commanding while following. A soldier who follows orders and sticks with her team to complete a mission has a higher survival rate. The team bond must be strong, and the value exchange between team members must be consistent for the safety of all. Forming teams that follow by leveraging individual strengths is a long-standing military leadership method that has shaped business leadership roles as well. The leader and the team must be in sync. The following paraphrases eleven leadership principles of the U.S. Marines:

1. Know yourself and seek self-improvement.
2. Be technically and tactically proficient.
3. Develop a sense of responsibility among your subordinates.
4. Make sound and timely decisions.
5. Set an example.
6. Know your people and look out for their welfare.
7. Keep your people informed.
8. Seek responsibility and take responsibility for your actions.
9. Ensure assigned tasks are understood, supervised, and accomplished.
10. Train your people as a team.
11. Employ your team in accordance with its capabilities.

(*Reference: http://www.au.af.mil/au/awc/awcgate/usmc/leadership.htm*)

It is up to you to lay out what successful performance looks like for you and your team. You are always in the middle, managing those you serve and those who serve you. Your style and value system are your foundation to convey to your team what matters. So, how do you facilitate creating the guiding principles of your team and how will you show up as a leader? You construct your rules of engagement and guiding principles in your early formation and when your team members change. Cohesive and collaborative communication informs your team's performance, and most importantly, it shows them how you plan to lead them.

▶ EXERCISE:

Team Operating Agreement—Rules of Engagement

This exercise is easier to manage with a facilitator, so I will give you the facilitation guidelines and show you examples of an end result where a team signs a contract to collaborate and hold up the principles of interaction. You can use this exercise for any level of team—project teams, departments, C-Suite leadership teams, and cross-functional leadership teams. It works for any group that comes together to serve their client base and internal staff.

EQUIPMENT/SUPPLIES
- Large Post-its that fit on an easel (2.5 ft. x 2.8 ft.). Make sure they can also stick to the wall.
- Index-sized Post-its
- Multiple colors of Sharpies

FACILITATION SETUP
- Schedule a sixty-minute meeting for the participating leadership team. Include a member from each department and try to keep the attendance to no more than nine people. (If more than nine people want to attend, you can run multiple groups.)
- Make sure you have a large conference room or space with blank walls where you can hang the large Post-its and have plenty of space to move around. You won't spend much time sitting.

FACILITATION
Step 1 — Introduction of the Exercise
Say this to your team:

In order to be a high-performing team, we are going to design an operating agreement/rules of engagement that will set a baseline for how we will show up and work together as a united front to serve our internal and external clients. Everyone in this room has a voice. Please use it so that you have a say in decision. We will run through a few steps to create a written agreement that we all will sign. When new team members join us, we will introduce them to these guiding principles and check in to see if the agreement needs to be updated based on our learning, and we will sign the agreement again. Let's begin.

Step 2 - Engagement

Ask the group:

- What are the characteristics you want others to see in this team? Write down your words on separate Post-its and put them up on one large Post-it on the wall labeled "Group characteristics/known for."
- What practices do we agree on and want to put in place regarding meeting management, ceremonies, and time commitment? Consider:
  - How do we start meetings? On time? How long? Note taking? Agenda driven? Phone use while in meeting? Frequency of meetings? How is it led? Action-item tracking? Post-meeting management?
  - How do you measure success of a meeting?
  - If there is a conflict, how will you resolve it in the meeting? Take a vote? Proposal/counterproposal? Tie-breaker methods? Rules?
  - How will you make sure all voices are heard?

End Result Example:

VXL Group

Operating Agreement

As a member of the VXL GROUP, I promise to exemplify the following characteristics, and I promise to be: Data Driven, Fun, Courageous, Innovative, Evangelical, Supportive, Value Oriented, Ruthless, Adventurous, Resourceful, Client/User-Centric, Bold, Collaborative, Innovative, Honest, Dedicated, Generous, Real, Passionate, Open-Minded, and Resilient.

When we commence a meeting, we will each abide by the following guidelines:

Running the Meeting

- Be present—no laptops/cell phones.
- If you are using technology, state why you are on it so the team understands.
- If technology is needed for use in the meeting, present the information or enable a video conference so that we can see each other, face to face, as much as possible.
- Conference rooms will be reserved to accommodate maximum attendance at meetings. If remote, must be stated ahead of the meeting so a dial-in is established.
- Come prepared, or request to reschedule the meeting if not prepared.
- If a member misses the meeting and wants to have her voice heard, she will either address it in the next meeting or ask a colleague to represent her point of view for coverage in the meeting.
- An agenda is always provided twenty-four hours prior to the meeting; otherwise, the meeting will be cancelled.
- Start on time/end on time.
- Post-meeting management: For continuous connectivity after the meeting and between meetings, utilize Slack for online communication or use the wiki to capture documentation and action items.
- Follow naming conventions determined by the team regarding collateral materials and documentation associated with products hosted on shared sites.
- Backlog management for the chapter will be managed in Jira; the voting system will be used to assist with prioritization. As a team member, I will respect the role the Backlog Gardner plays and abide by guidelines for backlog management outlined by the team.
- An Obstacle Board (blockers from getting our work done) will be created for items that cannot be directly resolved by the Product Management Chapter. Owners to help remove

the blocker and escalation paths to resolve the problem. TheObstacle Board will be reviewed prior to each chapter meeting to ensure awareness that action has been taken to resolve the issue or the item has been added to the agenda as a topic to review/discuss.

Meeting Cadence

- As a team, we agree to meet monthly with a concrete agenda outlined for each session.
- Agendas will be owned by the two Co-Chairs of the chapter, Stuart and Kareen. The Co-Chairs will determine prior to the meeting who will facilitate, present, take minutes, or be the timekeeper.
- Agenda will be distributed prior to the meeting and posted on a shared board for visibility during the meeting.
- Agendas will be outcome driven including, but not limited to, sharing breakthroughs and opportunities to continue to enhance the impact of the product management team within the organization.
- Every quarter, there will be a retrospective meeting to continue to enhance the chapter methods.
- Meeting hygiene actions will take place to consolidate or remove unnecessary meetings when duplication of efforts occurs or consolidation of agenda items can be leveraged.

Making Decisions/Managing Conflict

As a team member, I will use the "Time Out" hand signal when I think we need a reset on the conversation or to change the direction of the discussion. When I use the "Time Out" signal, I will propose what I believe the next action could be to move the meeting along or offer a proposal to resolve conflict. After I state my proposal, I will ask if there are any counterproposals. If there are no counterproposals, I will ask if everyone agrees with my original proposal. If *yes*, move on.

When there is a counterproposal, I can either amend an existing proposal or propose another option. The person taking notes for the meeting will scribe the proposals until they are all laid out.

When it's time to vote, the person taking notes will state the proposal and tally the votes across all options.

The team agrees that majority wins.

If there is a tie between two proposals, re-vote.

If there is not a distinct decision and the tie continues, the meeting facilitator will decide how the meeting should move forward and will assist the group to stay on agenda.

By signing below, I agree that I will be an upstanding member of the Product Management Chapter. I will abide by this operating agreement and speak up if I believe this needs to be updated once we start operating as a cohesive global team.

Signed by:

CHAPTER *Seven*

"Don't be intimidated by what you don't know. That can be your greatest strength and ensure that you do things differently from everyone else."

SARA BLAKELY, FOUNDER AND CEO OF SPANX

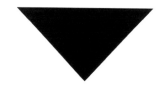

YOUR ORGANIZATIONAL VALUE SYSTEM

As you increase your responsibility at work, whether you've been promoted to lead more departments or you are sitting in the C-Suite leading the top executives of your firm, an Organizational Value System is at play. Your Organizational Value System is comprised of the individual values of each leader and the beliefs of the teams reporting to them as they show up and move forward together. When this value system includes strong, competing personalities and beliefs, the ripple effect across the organization is detrimental to business growth and sustainability of top performers. Focus first on your Personal Value System, next on your team, and finally to building a known value structure across your organization to create a system that you all understand. Without this crucial process, you are building your business on quicksand.

As Vice President of Operations for a communication application company, I experienced the importance for me to align my Personal Value System with the Organizational Value System in order to make strategic impact in the market. I was hired by the COO, who was young and ambitious and thrived on grooming companies for sale. He could then earn equity from the sale and move on to the next company. He hired for the gaps in his own skill set, so he could empower us as his direct reports to do what we do best. That was perfect for me because I love having the autonomy to leverage all that I know in new environments. My position required a Jackie of All Trades, and I was it. I oversaw daily operations for the firm, project management, engineering, and quality assurance for the app and web development teams. I had strong counterparts in marketing and product management, and we brought our teams together to drive delivery against the roadmaps we outlined. We built a team value system that increased the interest of clients for our product suite.

I kept my head down in assessment mode the first four to six weeks in this new leadership role. I highlighted the team strengths, the team weaknesses, how they aligned with the firm's overall strategy, and how the team aligned with the firm's culture. Overseeing the working environment and the technical delivery of the firm's products, I created working spaces that aligned the team atmosphere for high performance with the element of team transparency to understand what the team delivers, week over week. It was not easy to introduce change to an environment where mismanaged employees lacked leadership against a common goal. The original founders had been leading the firm for almost twenty years. They had their own way of commanding that aligned with their personal agenda, without much regard for the team. The team got away without advance planning or daily accountability. It was a reactionary environment, not a proactive one. The engineering team was resistant because they now reported to a woman who was two layers from the CTO to whom they previously reported. My work was cut out for me.

This environment lacked a strong leadership direction, and the staff was complacent. I knew I would be challenged at every turn by the people who reported to me, and the Founder/CEO didn't want to see things change. That was unsatisfying at best. I had to rely on my intelligence quotient (IQ) and emotional quotient (EQ) in order to enhance the processes and build a value exchange arena I would be proud to lead.

Within four months, the VP of Product Management and I put solid processes and training in place to build a cohesive, agile delivery and tracking process for each release across the technical stack. Clients were happier, and that resulted in more downloads, but internally, the C-Suite leaders did not include the two of us in their discussions. The CEO met us with animosity, anger, ego, and fear of losing control. He had been running the company with his buddy for almost twenty years. His processes were antiquated, but they worked for him and all the men he hired. He brought in the COO who hired me and the VP of Product Management to help ready the company to sell. If he could not sell the company, he would be out. Yet we were not included in pertinent leadership conversations, and that incited distrust across our team as the CEO went behind our backs to support a delivery agenda different from what we agreed to. The value system of the organization was out of alignment with mine. I felt completely devalued for all my efforts, and I considered leaving because the best possible outcome did not feel worth the fight.

I had attempted to build a cohesive work environment with common value exchange activities for my team and for my horizontal line of VPs. I felt disconnected from the Organizational Value System, because I was excluded from it and was not valued as a member of the leadership team. I checked in with my personal leadership vision: Where would I have the most impact, and what business model would allow me to create that impact for myself and others? Simultaneously, the VP of Product Management questioned her value in the firm and entertained an offer to join another firm. When I imagined leading in this environment without her and the potential impact on the Team Value System we had built, I saw a downward spiral into quicksand. If she left, I would have to resign, too.

At this point, monetary gain was not the only value in my Personal Value System. In my twenties, money was my means of survival to maintain my desired lifestyle. My position as the VP of Operations represented my capabilities, allowed me to build a solid infrastructure for delivery in alignment with my peers to steer the ship together. But there was a complete disconnect from the strategic growth, acceptance, and transparency I desired from the C-Suite team. As a female technology and operations leader, I had to watch my back and put on a masculine stance to leverage my intellect and people skills. Now, fifteen years in, I realized the organization would never align with my value structure or let me into its fold.

One week after my colleague resigned, I resigned, too. It was a risky decision, but I needed to put a stake in the ground and act for greater impact and alignment with my Personal Value System. This company was not a fit, and I wasn't willing to wait it out. I needed to protect myself and launch into the next phase of my career. I did help the COO find a replacement suitable for the team culture who would enjoy the challenges of working for the CEO. I was not the right fit, and it was time to launch my own business. I wanted to help multiple companies strategically grow as I, myself, continued to grow. The best Organizational Value System for me would be the one I could design and lead. Those who valued their investment in my time to be the expert in the room would hire me. The value exchange for me is knowing that I am uncompromising about my work for others. Being valued by those I serve is the highest reward I can receive.

Strategic Organizational Consulting

When I consult and coach companies for strategic growth, I facilitate to ensure the leadership team is built on inclusion to help drive the company's strategic goals. I have worked with top leaders to realign their team's skill set. Realignment might require restructuring, change in roles, or hiring new people to fill in the gaps, all with the view to align with the corporate culture and strategic growth delivery plans. For leaders to lead other leaders, they must understand the direction and agenda of each person working for them.

People you employ will always show up to follow; but if you empower them to lead, you will achieve your own leadership vision much faster.

The prior two exercises in this book gave you the tools to manage what you have control over as a team: yourself and the team that reports to you. Now it's time to up-level your skills for horizontal management. The leaders you work with to get things done within your firm face the same struggles you do. Define the value system you work within to ensure ease for your teams as they collaborate to achieve the firm's common strategic goals, and everyone wins. It is hard enough to manage what's already on your plate. That's why mastering what you do have control over and creating performance levels for yourself and your team will foster deeper engagement with your peer-level leaders.

To leverage the power of leadership across the executive level, you must articulate your personal values and raise awareness when your executive team values are out of alignment or need adjustment. That is the winning action to create a Value Exchange Leadership™ organization. Without defining your Organizational Value System, you cannot lead as a united front. Individual agendas will break down the advancement of your firm, and a whole segment of your company could be left behind or underutilized, which results in high expense to your firm. The leadership system across C-Suite and senior executives is a key component for potential business growth and scale to the next level. The leadership system will also demonstrate why things become stale and outgrown.

Recently, I worked with a CEO who had a strong desire to grow his business and build a legacy platform of income for his family. It was a twenty-year-old family-run business. This man had started the company from the ground up. They produced products for education systems and initially sold them through catalogs. Then they moved into ecommerce to expand their reach. He worked with one of my vendor partners to deliver enhancements to his digital marketing strategies, when he realized their business strategy wasn't strong enough to achieve their monetary goals. My vendor partner told him, "Speak to Kareen Walsh. She is an expert in mapping out growth strategies and aligning the right organizational structure to help you scale with ease." He followed through and called me.

I could tell in our initial call that this CEO had great ambition, a dream to build a multimillion-dollar company, and a leadership stance based on a fear of change that hindered his growth. I proposed a coaching/consulting program that combined (a) a brand strategy for growth by my brand strategist expert and (b) direct work with me to align operations, leadership, and technology to take them to the next level of desired growth. He accepted the proposal, and I began my assessment.

I looked under the hood of the organization to see how he ran it, staffed it, and empowered his team and leaders. I discovered a breakdown between his Organizational Value System and his Personal Value System. That breakdown held him back from building the legacy revenue he desired. The most challenging part of aligning the systems was to affect major behavioral change. That would be hard for a leader of his stature to swallow. Working through EQ imbalances is the most challenging part of reshaping a leader, but it is a worthwhile investment that makes real change happen. Good intentions are one thing, but if you don't act on them, they are just unfulfilled dreams.

This CEO had achieved a lot on his own. He was a skilled engineer. He loved numbers, analyzing data, and creating spreadsheets to prove the value of his business. Until ecommerce and online shopping became common—about fifteen years into his business— he didn't have significant competition. In the last five years, however, he had invested more in updating the infrastructure of his technology than in leveraging marketing and sales tactics to build a buying market that would scale. His competitors had come out with similar products at a lower price. He needed new tactics, strategies, and the operations to back up the volume of sales it would take to hit the multimillion-dollar goal he planned to achieve by 2020.

I have said it before, and I will say it again: If you are not growing as a leader, your business will not grow. I recognized this CEO's limitations in skill and his desire to run his business and invest in the soft skills required to build the company to the size he wanted. He wanted the results without the effort.

I advised him to try incremental changes in order to build the consistency required on the digital marketing side of the house. I showed him how a shift in behavior—empowering others to do what he doesn't have the skills for–will boost his business. He was a half-baked CEO who made sure his staff got paid and his products got sold, but his approach to sell more was always to offer a discount to his buyers. That is not scalable for overall growth. His leadership stance needed an overhaul. Some of his strongest team members were starting to leave. He hired family members to help build an income, but he never offered training on the skills they needed to do the job. It was hard to present growth opportunities for him to launch with a strawman team. As the numbers dwindled month over month, his stress levels rose. That put him in a reactionary space of controlling. He reverted to old habits of what he knew, rather than following through on the activities we discussed.

His Personal Value System:
  – Family First, Responsibility, Stability, Ownership
His Organizational Value System:
  – Responsiveness, Inclusion, Status Quo
These are solid foundational values. But when you want to scale, the values of change, evolution, and growth need to be in the mix; otherwise, your business will flatline.

My team put together great recommendations to scale the business. But, first, organization and leadership needed to change. This CEO was not yet ready for those changes. He was so stressed about the lack of earnings month over month and so worried about making payroll that he could not follow through on any major changes across his organization. This fear-based approach would hold the business at status quo, rather than growing toward the arbitrary goals for 2020. At least now, the sounding board of an outsider's view revealed the shortcomings incumbent in lack of follow-through and gave him a more realistic direction. It was deflating, but this is a common occurrence when a strategy is built on pie-in-the-sky numbers without commitment to what it takes to run a business at that scale. The other obstacle in this organization was this Founder/CEO's discomfort in operating his business—he did not step into the ownership role to empower the appropriate leaders to do what they do best. Until he could change his behavior, the company growth plan would never come to fruition.

I would not end our contractual obligation without adding value and steering him toward growth. We delivered a brand strategy for his digital marketing team to attract and engage their primary target audience. We helped staff a new Director of Marketing to manage daily marketing tactics for consistency in sales across their existing product suite. We mapped out directional changes to implement in the future, once they were back in the green. I outlined what a scaled organizational structure would look like for his firm, the type of leaders he would need to hire to build it, and processes to ensure he continuously produced products his clients demanded in order to differentiate them from their competitors. He was not yet ready to invest in the strategies we proposed. He realized he had to reset his goals. When he is ready to move forward with either scaling the business or closing it down, I will walk alongside him in his decision. What is certain is that the business will only grow at the pace he, himself, chooses to grow.

Up-Leveling Value Systems at the Organizational Level

I have worked with and for organizations with territorial leaders who think only of their own agenda, their own department, and their own wins. They resort to finger-pointing when other departments do not support their need to succeed. They create a ripple effect of finger-pointing throughout their department, which leads to a broken value exchange organization and affects the rules of engagement between cross-functional teams. These heads of organization do not see the value in leveraging the needs and demands of other departments to find the win. Those departments are then run so that performance measurements and promotions are based on following versus leading toward strategic goals. That C-Suite member rewards others who behave like he does—his value system is accepted in that environment. Luckily, as individuals, we get to choose what value system we want to be a part of.

A thriving organization where cohesive collaboration aligns with the Organizational Value System is beautiful. It is a rare occurrence when leaders at the C-Suite level conduct their operations based on value. When they do, the firm as a whole rises to the top of the best places to work, their client base is filled with raving fans, and individuals in the system are on a performance growth path to become leaders within the firm.

Organizational Value System Exercise

How do you create or evaluate if the value exchange system of your organization is right for you? My favorite way to see if cross-functional leaders are aligned is to get a group of their direct reports into a room and run a retrospective on how they operate as a cross-functional team. This is best done by a third-party facilitator, someone who is not tied to the outcome and won't sway the information addressed by the cross-functional team.

I learned about facilitating retrospectives when I became a Certified SCRUM Master (CSM). I learned to facilitate agile teams to deliver high-quality products by being cohesive, collaborative, and able to pivot when the direction of their work was not in sync with the demands of the client base. A retrospective is a ceremonial meeting facilitated at the end of a segment of development. The purpose is to check in as a team and apply any changes that will enhance the delivery of the project and the team's ability to work together.

I use the retrospective with leadership teams and business partners because it is the quickest way to gauge what is working, what needs to stop, and what needs to change. It ends with an action plan. Conducting this for a leadership team is a bit different because you want to give everyone a voice without being dominated by whom they report to. Read through this whole exercise to prepare and conduct with your team.

▶ EXERCISE:
Retrospective for Leadership Teams

EQUIPMENT/SUPPLIES
- Large Post-its that fit on an easel (2.5 ft. x 2.8 ft.). Make sure they can also stick to the wall.
- Index-sized Post-its.
- Multiple colors of Sharpies.

FACILITATION SETUP
- Schedule a sixty-minute meeting for the participating leadership team. Include a member from each department and try to keep the attendance to no more than nine people. (If more than nine people want to attend, you can run multiple groups.)
- Make sure you have a large conference room or space with blank walls where you can hang the large Post-its and have plenty of space to move around. You won't spend much time sitting.

FACILITATION
Step 1—Introduction of the Exercise

Say to your team:

I have called this meeting with cross-functional leaders to assess how we are doing as a Value Exchange Leadership™ group. What I have learned from Kareen Walsh, Founder and Creator of the VXL Coaching and Training Programs, is that if we don't focus on the value exchange between our teams and our clients, we are not leveraging the potential of our firm's capabilities and strategic growth. This exercise will help us identify what is working really well, what we should probably stop doing, and what we should start doing. Then we can devise a plan to move forward.

Here are the ground rules or this to work. All input is accepted and welcomed. No judgment will be made on your suggestions and recommendations; we will just put it to a vote of importance by the group before we act. If at any point there is a debate or conversation that eats away at our time for today, and if I think it requires an offline discussion, I will call it out, and we will put it on the parking-lot list. (Point to parking-lot list—a blank large Post-it on the wall behind you.) If you accept these terms of facilitation today and are willing to put your best into this exercise, please raise your cell phone in your right hand and hand it to me for safekeeping during this exercise. (Wink at them and put their phones aside.)

Our time in this meeting is limited for a reason—I want it to be an effective use of your time, and I also know that the brilliance in this room will help us identify where we stand and what we are willing to do going forward. Are you ready to get started? Everyone grab a small Post-it pad and a Sharpie.

Step 2—What Is Going Well

Ask the group:

What does our organization do really well?

- Leading others (2 minutes)

- Helping our teams grow (2 minutes)
- Helping each other grow (2 minutes)
- Building strong cross-functional operations (2 minutes)
- Serving our clients (2 minutes)

Place three large Post-its on the wall with a happy face in the top left corner and ask your group to start placing their small Post-its on the large Post-its. *Don't review the information posted until Step 4 of this exercise.*

Step 3—What Do We Need to Stop Doing

Ask the group:

What does our organization need do stop doing that hinders us from:

- Leading others (2 minutes)
- Helping our teams grow (2 minutes)
- Helping each other grow (2 minutes)
- Building strong cross-functional operations (2 minutes)
- Serving our clients (2 minutes)

Place three large Post-its on the wall with a sad face in the top left corner and ask your group to start placing their small Post-its on the large Post-its.

Step 4–Review

You, the facilitator, will review what has been posted that is supporting and what has been posted that is hindering performance. This makes everyone aware of what has been shared. Then ask each member to vote on the top three things they do really well that defines the value system of the organization and the top three things they believe should be stopped in order to increase the value exchange across the team. Have them cast their votes by putting a line or a dot with their Sharpie on each Post-it they are voting for.

Pull the top three Post-its for the Support and Hinder lists and put them on a new large Post-it with the Delta sign (triangle) at the top (which stands for change).

Step 5—What Do We Need to Start Doing

- On new Post-its write three proposals/actions that you think we should start doing to increase our value exchange performance between departments and as an organization. It can be an enhancement to what we do really well, but it can also focus on how to solve what is hindering us from leading at our highest potential. Keep the top-voted items in mind as you propose actions for change.
- Use the top-voted "Hinder" Post-its as your guide while the team is writing down proposed solutions. Repeat what they say on those cards so creativity can flow across the team (7 minutes).
- Have them put their Post-its for change on the large Delta Post-it.

Step 6—Review and Action Plan (15 minutes)

- Read the solutions out loud, so everyone knows what is being proposed.
- Ask everyone to vote on the top three solutions they think will move the needle in the value exchange organizational system by putting a line or a dot with their Sharpie on each Post-it they are voting for.
- Now is the time to own and act. Read the top three voted solutions for the group. In order to take action, someone from this group must lead the change. If this group doesn't act, change won't happen. Ownership does not mean doing all the work yourself; it means you own the mission of change behind the card that has the highest votes. You are volunteering to lead and follow up with this group to make sure the cross-functional teams take action together. Value exchange cannot be one-sided.
- Pick the highest-voted item first and ask who in the room wants to own leading this mission to see this change

happen. Do the same for two more of the highest-voted items and have a leader volunteer to own it.

- In the last few minutes of the meeting, have each leader who "owned" a card write down one action to take between now and the next time you meet. Make sure there is a "by when" date on each action. Examples:
  o Review the issue and proposed solution with C-Suite management team to get buy-in by 11/15/2018.
  o Form a cross-functional management team across all departments to outline possibilities of change toward this proposed solution by 11/01/2018.
  o Follow up with this group on proposed next action steps for this solution by 10/31/2018.

Step 7—Thank You

Thank everyone for coming, pick a date and time for the next meeting, and document all notes, Post-its, and actions to share with them in the meeting notes that will be posted/sent to them for reference.

You can repeat this exercise as many times as needed, at any level of leadership, until you start to see the impact to your Organizational Value System. Hint: If this meeting only happens once and is an epic fail with a lack of communication, input, and ownership, that is a sign of the current value system. That awareness allows you to decide if it aligns with your Personal Value System to stick around.

CHAPTER
Eight

"If your actions inspire others to dream more,

learn more, do more and become more,

you are a leader."

JOHN QUINCY ADAMS

ARE YOU AN EFFECTIVE LEADER?

How do you gauge effectiveness? Some leadership styles can push the needle or increase your bottom line. Effectiveness depends on how you lead in your given circumstances: how you show up under stress and in moments of celebration; how you build a team and hire top performers; how you collaborate with them all against a strategy to deliver. You probably have more examples of what an effective leader IS NOT, right? Maybe you reported in to someone and questioned if they understood what was happening because their direction was so off the mark. Or they piled tasks, challenges, obstacles, and basically their whole job onto you. Or C-Suite leaders who pulled numbers together that looked good to the board but didn't reflect how the company was actually doing—yet they acted as if they had it all together. And when the board or investors bought into that pro forma, you had to pressure your team to deliver against it. It is effective for financial gain for the firm but can be completely disruptive on how the people of that firm are managed and valued. This displays an organizational value system that may or may not be aligned with your team or personal value system, which is a dynamic to assess in order to understand the overall effectiveness of leadership in this echo-system.

Effectiveness is subjective because it carries the weight of other people's views to determine if your style is a fit for the culture. Determine your style by understanding your Personal Value System, articulating your deal breakers, and articulating the highest standard of how you choose to lead. If you don't know what you value, no one else will. Effective leadership stems from the behaviors we embody when our Personal Value System is aligned or off-balance. When it is aligned, we are in our most creative space. We can lead with integrity, self-awareness, and empathy; and we easily empower those who work for and with us when we understand their value system. We are all a part of the whole. You cannot lead alone.

The assessment tool I use to gauge leadership effectiveness combines the feedback from those you work with, work for, and work alongside to reveal how you show up in your creative space and your reactive space.

How Do You Define Effective Leadership

Effective leadership consists of many factors. Understanding your Personal Value System, the Organizational Value System, and where you are aligned will impact your leadership effectiveness. I use the "Leadership Circle 360 Profile" (TLC360) assessment tool because it provides data for a leader from the people they work with, for, and alongside. The leader then compares it with their self-assessment. The result is a map that shows gaps between how they think they show up and how others perceive them. The map helps me (as coach) and them (as leaders) to determine where they thrive, how effective they are, and what needs improvement for them to become the leader they envision being.

When I first used this assessment tool, the results map impressed me. It pinpointed how I was showing up, as well as my effectiveness in my leadership environment. The difference between my perception of myself and my team's perception of me was remarkable. The output was so impressive, I had to use it with my clients. I became certified to use this tool because it was the most comprehensive data set that allowed me to help my leaders jump into action to be more effective.

The TLC360 breaks down how a person shows up in their creative and reactive spaces. It shows the effectiveness of a person's leadership style. Time and time again, people take on roles they want to play, but they don't look at the skill set or qualifications required to be effective in the role. I help leadership teams and C-Suite executives identify their style and own how they show up. But, most of all, I help them clarify what is effective for them and for their team to create the corporate culture they desire.

One CEO of a small firm, when under stress, would lean into a reactive space, which proved destructive and impacted his leadership effectiveness. I helped him identify that by looking at the results of the TLC360 assessment. It was not his intention to close off his team and make them feel less-than from his outbursts, so he needed a way to manage his reactions and be more effective under stress.

Leading others and serving clients carries big responsibility. I teach my clients how to compartmentalize their reactions based on the audience and what's at stake. The founder and CEO of a company has more emotional connection to her work than an employee of someone else's firm in a senior role.

It takes passion to run your own company. But emotional outbursts that put other people down or make them feel small is uncalled for. It creates a dynamic of distrust and fear-ridden communication among team members. You will build your company on false ground because people are afraid to tell you the truth. Avoidance is another emotional extreme. Lack of communication around hard topics can stem from surprising or disappointing emotions. For instance, if something makes you want to cry when you talk about it, you may hesitate to share your truth in fear that you will be perceived as "weak." Your withholding engenders distrust from your team because they see the avoidance. They just want to stop digging a deeper hole in an unsatisfying direction.

I discussed trigger management with my CEO client. Identifying the triggers that create a volatile emotional response is key to addressing the situation with a valid response versus an inflated one. It requires discipline to master this, but it's worth it if your current reactions are not adding value and only make you less effective as a leader.

▶ EXERCISE:

STEP 1—PAUSE AND TAKE INVENTORY OF WHAT MAKES YOU RETREAT INTO YOUR REACTIVE SPACE.

The tool summarizes three main categories as reactive spaces: complying, protecting, and controlling. Understanding your reactive space helps you better understand the triggers that put you there. That self-awareness helps you know why you react so quickly. The creative space you thrive in pulls you out. When you pause and assess the events, you can compartmentalize what is true and what triggers an old, repeated story that makes you react negatively.

STEP 2—SEPARATE THE ISSUE/PROBLEM FROM THE EMOTION. WHAT IS REALLY BEING SAID, DONE, OR ASKED FOR?

Write out the issue/request and identify the source of your reaction as you hear it. Is it a loss of business? Is it a personality conflict? Is it idiotic? Is it a repeat of something you thought had passed? Write it down, then ask yourself:

- What outcome really matters to me if this were solved?
- Is my emotional reaction about the issue or about the person delivering the message?
- What are the top three questions I need answered to solve this with ease?

STEP 3—SHARE YOUR TRUTH WITH YOUR TEAM.

Share your findings from Step 2.

- This is what matters to me regarding the issue.
- This is how I feel about it.
- This is what I need answered to help us all move forward.

Here's the deal: People all have different levels of emotional intelligence. Honor that. We all serve a purpose as part of a whole. We all have past stories that trigger us, excite us, and shut us down. We have all lived through a pain story. We all react when the shit hits the fan.

Wouldn't it be easier if you knew at least half of this up front when working with your team or organization? Wouldn't it be easier if you could hold space for people in their time of stress and help them push through it versus elevating your stress and shutting down? Imagine knowing exactly how to resolve conflict and misunderstanding in minutes versus letting it fester for days to affect the overall performance of your team, your business, and your bottom line. When you articulate what is going on with you and approach your reaction with authentic forward motion, you help others understand how best to communicate with you. That builds trust. And the next time shit hits the fan, your behavior will help others manage with ease together.

Don't use the excuse of time to avoid practicing these tools. We are all busy. But do you want to be busy creating more chaos, or do you want to be busy creating growth for you and your company? Start with communication. When you know how you all operate and react when shit hits the fan, you will grow faster with fewer growing pains. You can avoid the weight of reactive miscommunication that drags your team down. Hit it head-on and create a space that welcomes forward-thinking honesty, and you avoid the resultant poor decisions.

All members in the Value Exchange Leadership™ 90-Day Mastermind participate in TLC360, so each leader understands his effectiveness today and how best to map out actions to be even more effective going forward. This clarity on personal style is a game changer for leaders. It's enlightening to see how it aligns with their Personal Value System to enhance their impact in the world.

● ● ● ● ● ●

For more information or to access the brochure that outlines the TLC360 tool, go to:
https://www.kareenwalsh.com/leadership-assessment-tool.

● ● ● ● ● ●

Two Rules to Live By to Increase Your Effectiveness

Two things ARE NOT effective for value exchange: assumption and avoidance. Here are two simple rules to follow as a value exchange leader.

RULE #1: DO NOT ASSUME YOUR TEAM KNOWS YOUR AGENDA. VOCALIZE IT.

The number one problem I see with ineffective leaders is a break-down in communication regarding expectations from direct reports. I've met with direct reports who are clueless as to the actual objective for all the work on their plate because their boss hasn't articulated it. When I speak to their boss, I find that communication has been minimal. It's a palm-to-face moment because it represents assumption-based communication. *I assume my team can read my mind, therefore I don't have to explain it.* Honestly, it happens more with leaders who have no clue what they are meant to achieve. They avoid their team because they don't know where they are leading them. It's as effective as herding cats. Follow Rule #1 and don't be afraid to tell your team you don't know. Informing your team lets the air out of the tension bubble and changes complacency to engagement. Let them know exactly where you are and what's needed, so they can be of value to you in the process.

RULE #2: DON'T BRING YOUR TEAM DOWN BY AVOIDING THE UNKNOWN.

Avoidance is the worst response when you are unsure of your personal path or the direction your team is headed. Unless you are the owner of the company, your role is to fulfill your assigned job. If you are unsure of your direction and your value to the firm based on the Organizational Value System of the leaders you report to, your duty is to manage your role and responsibilities with your boss. That gives you and your team clarity. In leadership, you are never alone. If you don't know, ask for help, clarity, or guidance to push through the unknown and lead. Avoidance trickles down to your team. When they see you avoiding due to discomfort, they feel permission to do the same. If your team performs out of complacency versus growth, look in the mirror. What do you need to stop avoiding, before it gets worse?

Focus on these two rules when your team performs inadequately or if your company is not growing. Facing up to this problem, rather than avoiding it or assuming things about it, turns the whole thing around. First, admit it to yourself. Second, go through the following checklist to pinpoint the breakdown and increase your effectiveness by clearly defining what needs to shift.

▶ EXERCISE:
Assumption Checklist

To add value, identify if you know for sure what is happening or if you are merely assuming. If any of the following are true, you are assuming, and you know what they say about assuming (Ass – U – Me). A leader who assumes is an ass.

- You haven't had a one-on-one with your direct reports in more than ten days, and you assume they are on task for their deliverables.
- You haven't had a one-on-one with your boss, and you assume he knows what you are working on based on an email you sent him. (Verbal understanding and written understanding are two different things.)
- It's been more than thirty days since you had a team meeting to reiterate the focus and reasons for team initiatives.
- Project initiative tracking is all over the place, and there isn't one consistent view that puts a finger on the pulse of delivery across the team.
- You have verbal assessment from direct reports but have not seen solid proof of their stated outcomes.
- It's been more than thirty days since you engaged with your customer base to see how your products or services are performing.
- You believe your direct reports have informed their teams of the department strategy, but you haven't addressed the teams directly to confirm it.

Avoidance Checklist

Use the following list to determine if you are adding value or avoiding something that needs immediate attention.

- You haven't had a one-on-one with your direct reports in the last ten days.
- You haven't met with your boss in the last ten days.
- You haven't had a C-Suite meeting to discuss the state of the business in the last ten days.
- It's been more than thirty days since you sent a message to all members of your department regarding the strategy and performance of the overall team's initiatives.

- You haven't delivered a project of impact in the last thirty days.
- You are showing up late to meetings, rather than owning how you manage your time.
- You are showing up late to work, because you don't want to face the day.

Eliminate assumption and avoidance and watch your team and your company thrive.

► CHAPTER
Nine

"Leadership is about empathy.
It is about having the ability to relate to and
connect with people for the purpose of
inspiring and empowering their lives."

OPRAH WINFREY, CEO AND FOUNDER OF THE OWN NETWORK

VALUE EXCHANGE LEADERSHIP™ IN ACTION

You reflect your team, just as they reflect you. If you don't know what they value and you find yourself questioning their behavior or if you get negative feedback from other people regarding their approach, remember that they reflect you. They could be showing up based on something they learned or something that is condoned under your management. It is important for a leader to consistently check in with a set agenda to stay on top of the team's current goals and obstacles. At the same time, you must understand what they value most. That way you can assess how best to motivate them when it gets hard and how to reward them when they have completed the task. (Rewards come in all forms, only one of which is money.) Here's an agenda to follow with direct reports to keep you in the know and to support them in their endeavors.

Schedule weekly thirty-minute one-on-ones with your direct reports. Include an agenda in each weekly invitation. This is the time to check in on progress against their strategic project assignments, help them remove obstacles that block their goals, and understand more deeply what they want to achieve under your direction. It is completely okay to befriend your employees and to mingle outside of the workplace to build a bond, but it is not okay to be in the "friend" state of mind in every business interaction. You are their leader, and they look to you for guidance. If you don't know your own path and can't articulate your own goal, then you are only *managing* the current situation, not *leading* it. Do you see the difference? Managers maintain the status quo. Leaders enhance it, turn it on its head, and optimize results for the ultimate outcome. Which one are you?

Nothing makes you a better leader than engaging with your direct reports about how best to lead them. Ask them what they need, help them identify their personal career goals, and support them in achieving the required skill set to carry that out. Make sure they're recognized within the firm and bolster their confidence to ask for the next seat they desire. You can't do that for others if you haven't done it for yourself. Self-starters don't need others to show them how; they do it themselves and lead the way. If you need someone to guide you, use me as your avatar leader. Following is an example that demonstrates how your recognition of their values empowers your direct reports to show up for you in the face of challenge. Trust that they will perform in kind.

When I was twenty-seven, I became the Senior Leader of Mergers and Acquisition Operations. I reported to the VP of Technology, who never took the time to understand my views or recognize my methods as valuable. He led from his arrogance. It didn't really matter to me at the time because I was close with the CTO and knew that if I needed anything, I had a direct line to her as my guide. My direct boss was a manager, not a leader. I had outgrown his skill set to help me grow within the firm. I was respectful, I showed up for him, and I swallowed my reactions to his condescension. I knew that fighting him would get me nowhere. Some days I was strong and could take it. Other days I felt angry and went to the gym to let it all out, crying because he was so hurtful and unaware of his impact. Since I would have to go through him to advance, I knew I would not last long at the firm. The only roles possible for me there held no promise of satisfaction for me.

While enduring this style of management, I focused on what I could control—my team and their growth, our clients and their success, and my personal plan for what I wanted next. I became a stronger communicator with my team because a string of male leaders loved my operational mind and my ability to execute, but to move forward, anything I did had to be their idea. I had to pick my battles. Despite their condescening words and actions, I showed up respectfully with solutions instead of complaints. I would have to swallow my pride at times to get through certain meetings and leverage my EQ to manuver their IQ. It was my best effort to manage upwards. When some leaders treated me badly and my emotions started to take over, I would focus on the issues at hand, suppressing my anger or sadness in that environment. I always tried to lead my team by the example I wished for myself. I showed my team the empathy, care, and guidance that I hoped for from a leader and demonstrated that what I valued was possible.

One of my direct reports, an amazing taskmaster like myself, had a sweet disposition. She showed up when asked, but she had personal challenges that resulted in confusion about her career goals and what to do next. In the three months I had been her direct manager, we built a strong rapport. I consistently held one-on-ones to get the lay of the land of the team, the operations to date, the obstacles we faced, and where we needed to avoid excessive overhead. I made time to get to know her better and learn what motivated her. I learned she was burned out by the lack of leadership and direction she had received until now. She felt disheartened and neglected. Her ability to hold the team and operations together without much support had gone unnoticed. She hadn't had a raise or promotion for her efforts in two years.

I learned that she loved animals, that she was dating someone new, and that she carried the weight of a divorce settlement from the year prior. She had a sister and brother she adored and divorced parents who had issues communicating. She was vegetarian. Knowing all of this helped me understand what brought her joy and what stressed her out.

We did one-on-ones as "Walk and Talks" on the Embarcadero by the San Francisco Bay. It got us out of the office for fresh air and fresh solutions to our new challenges. A change of environment brings a change of perspective. On one walk, after we caught up on the work happenings, I asked her, "What role in life would make you excited to jump out of bed every morning?"

She responded with hesitation, but she trusted me to hear her response. "I would love to work with animals every day and help them heal through their pain."

I responded with support that she did not expect. "You should look into how you can do that. If you are not doing what you are passionate about, you are not living."

I knew that she was doing her current job because she was *qualified*, not because she was *passionate* about it. I knew that if she had the space to express what she really wanted, she would find a way to achieve it. I also knew that if her current job was not satisfying, she would not grow in her role. That would be a disservice to those who reported to her because they would never grow, either. Her lack of enthusiasm would translate into lack of opportunity for those who did want to be there and grow within the firm. It was my responsibility to create opportunity for my team to grow, even if it meant losing the employee. You can always replace taskmasters, but grooming leaders is not so easy. You must understand their passion in order to groom them for leadership and success. Someone whose passion for animals remains a hobby while she toughs it out to build data reconciliation teams will be less than her best in either field. It's a dead end for everyone.

Here's how Value Exchange Leadership™ shows up in action. A few weeks after that conversation, we had our one-on-one. We identified wins of the last two weeks and obstacles to remove. I asked, "What can I help you achieve this week? How can I be of service?" She said, "Kareen, I found a program to become an animal massage therapist. It is an immersion week, and I would like to use my vacation days to attend the training." AMAZING! I responded, "Show me how you will have your work covered before you go and have a blast!"

Her desired training had nothing to do with our company or our line of business. But here's the value it brings to the table for her as my direct report and for me as her boss: It aligned her with who she wants to be in her everyday life, which meant she would show up for work with more vigor and focus. It created opportunities that thrilled her, even while working in an arena that didn't quite do it for her. It also gave me time to meet one-on-one with her direct reports while she was out for the week, to understand what they valued, and to assess who might a be good replacement, just in case this woman wanted to leave and pursue her passion full time.

There's no future in having people working for you who don't want to be there. When the energy of one brings down the many, the system is devalued. Direct reports who have managerial titles and responsibilities set the tone for the rest of the team. If the team members who work for you are merely collecting their checks and not actively moving the business forward, you have a complacent environment that will not grow. And that falls on you as the leader. It is up to you to know where you are headed and where your direct reports want to be. When you harness that energy and cultivate a space of learning each other's innate values and desires, you can lead them forward or lead them out.

If you don't know what passion drives your direct reports, schedule a one-on-one with each right now and use this agenda for your conversation. Don't judge their answers. Simply create the space for them to express freely. Start the conversation by sharing your passion. You can even say, "I just read the book *Lead with Value* by Kareen Walsh. She tells how she helped her direct reports pursue their personal goals while working for her. I realized that I have never shared with you what I feel passionate about, and I would love to hear the same from you. Let's figure out how to help you accomplish that. Even if it is outside this work arena, I can help you accomplish your desired skills as you work toward what is next. I value you on the team, and for me to understand you, I need to know your passion and if there is a role you want to play to fulfill it."

How would if feel if the person you reported to did this for you? Would you show up differently? If you are in a C-Suite seat and haven't checked in with yourself on this, have a meeting with your other C-Suite members for each to answer this question. You hold each other up. You are in this together. It's not "us versus them" in organizational leadership. Imagine the collective leadership strength when your colleagues know each other's passion. Your passion directly correlates with your highest values. Understand this about who works for you and who you work with, and the exchange between you will be easy and satisfying. It will translate automatically to your clients and will positively impact your bottom line.

Agendas for One-on-Ones
Here are some agenda guidelines to add value to your leadership style and team.

AGENDA FOR VALUE EXCHANGE LEADERSHIP™ ONE-ON-ONE
(Weekly, 30 Minutes)

Schedule a set time with your direct reports each week and stick to it. Make them feel important and show up for them.

- What wins do you have to share this week?
- What are your challenges/obstacles?
- How can I assist?

AGENDA FOR ONBOARDING NEW DIRECT REPORTS
(60 Minutes within the first week you work together)

When you onboard a new direct report, it is critical that your cadence of communication be consistent and value-driven to help them jump in and run with the goals you have set for them. In your first one-on-one:

- Ask: What is your approach in a new job, and how can I best guide you to build certainty in your role here?
- Ask: What is your preferred method of learning (audio, visual, written)? I want to send you the right resources to understand the landscape of our firm and team.
- Lay out the setup for their first projects, the challenges you want them to focus on, the strategy or service that your team offers, and where you stand today in relationship to it all. Say what you want them to accomplish. (Don't assume that your initial interview covered all they need to know to provide value. Reiterate it.)
- Provide a list of people they should meet with one-on-one to get the landscape of the organization.
- Define the cadence of when and how you two will meet and the agenda moving forward.
- Schedule the next one-on-one immediately. For some new direct reports, doing a daily stand-up helps them gain positive momentum.

AGENDA FOR QUARTERLY VALUE EXCHANGE LEADERSHIP™ CHECK-IN
(40 Minutes within the first week you work together)

This is where you learn how they are doing overall and understand what they have learned and what they want to pursue. Share your goals and what you are pursuing to assess if what they want is something you are ready to release to them. Use the retrospective format for your quarterly meetings.

- What has gone well that you want to continue doing?
- What should we stop doing?
- What should we start doing to help you inch toward your goals?
- What are the top three actions to focus on this quarter?
- Relay your progress as a leader and your focus. What can you give them that aligns with their top three actions? (This may not be relevant every quarter, but I guarantee it will be relevant in at least one.)

Take and store your own notes for each one-on-one you conduct. It will make your performance review process easier, and because you won't have to rack your brain for tangible results during a yearly interview, it will help you easily advance people under your leadership. As value exchange leader, you will be in the know about each person's performance because you keep it top of mind in your consistent interactions. Even if your organization is not quite at Value Exchange Leadership™ levels, nothing stops you from building your organization to reflect your leadership style. The one thing you are always in control of as a leader is how you show up for those who report to you.

▶ CHAPTER
Ten

"I've learned that people will forget what you said, people will forget what you did, but people will never forget how you made them feel."

MAYA ANGELOU, AUTHOR, POET, AND THOUGHT LEADER

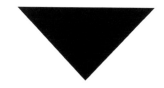

BE A VALUE EXCHANGE LEADER

You now understand your personal vision and value system; you have facilitation methods to build your team and organizational value system; and you know how you show up as a value exchange leader.

What next? How do you consistently put this learning into action? How do you attract a tribe of other value exchange leaders to build high-performing teams and companies together? How can you tell if the company you want to move into next has this value structure intact?

Leaders don't hesitate; they act.

If reading this book makes you realize you are more of a manager than a leader, that's a good thing! Most managers don't know how to lead. They learn how as they expose themselves to new leadership methods and others who have mastered them. If you have been leading from your reactive space versus your creative space, and if that has made you more self-aware and clarified your vision for the type of leader you strive to be, congratulations! This is a foundational step to drive value into all that you do. In turn, it raises your self-awareness because you are now dialoguing with your direct reports and clients at a new level, meeting their needs as well as yours. Whether you are a self-appointed C-Suite leader having co-founded your company or you inherited a family business, you have gained a new skill to include your direct reports and your C-Suite team into a value-based dialogue. You can grow past your limitations and help those who report to you grow. Your leadership vision will manifest quickly now. What a gift!

To go deeper with the teachings in this book, I launched the Value Exchange Leadership 90-Day Mastermind. This program assures you are not alone in your journey, and it provides space for the clarity you need on your next steps. It also gives you the space to practice without being judged if you now realize that your Organizational Value System is not aligned with your Personal Value System. This program will help you change that and determine if your next step is to plan an exit strategy, or if you will leverage these tools to refine the Organizational Value System within your current firm.

I understand where you are, and you are not alone. My mission is to walk alongside you until you outrun me. When you are ready for that next level, call me again, and I will be right by your side.

My Personal Value System is based on high-quality service with a combination of empathy, understanding, and strategic action to make positive impact on the companies that hire me. I first had to master my leadership style, so I could assist you with your own. I continue to learn new methods, and they all are founded in understanding what is most valuable in each moment to each person involved. With that understanding, we can act appropriately for the most valuable outcome for the whole. We can use multiple tactics based on the people involved and the environment in which they work. Regardless of the factors at hand, the result is value-ridden because that was our focus and understanding from the beginning. With value-based systems, failures don't hit so hard. Acting from value rather than greed allows forward momentum to continue, and our failures are forgiven.

My goal is to continue to impact the methods of leadership groups, because if I can help one leader perform better and be more fulfilled, those who surround him or her will also benefit. I hope you have received at least one actionable Value Exchange Leadership™ tool that will propel you forward. When you are ready to go deeper and connect with the VXL tribe, apply for an exclusive seat in the Value Exchange Leadership 90-day Master-mind. It would be my honor to work with you.

ACKNOWLEDGMENTS

Thank you to the leaders who have gone before me and showed me the way. Thank you to the trainers and coaches, David T. S. Wood, Chris Harder, Lori Harder, Tony Robbins, Lisa Nichols, Gabby Bernstein, Bob Anderson, Lyssa Adkins, Brené Brown, and John Maxwell, who have taught me how to get out of my comfort zone and stretch my level of understanding, so I can be a better servant leader to my team and my clients.

I thank my husband for his continuous support of my personal and professional growth. He has helped me go further than I ever could have imagined.

Especially, thank you to my clients who have trusted me as a resource and allowed me to walk alongside them in their badass journey to becoming the best value exchange leaders in action in their arenas of expertise.

AN INVITATION

If this book inspires you to learn more and interact with a community of like-minded leaders, visit www.kareenwalsh.com/leadwithvalue.

Connect with the group of brilliant people who lead with value every day and who want to connect and serve, just like you. That exchange is valuable and powerful!

In appreciation for the value you share by picking up this book, I extend a special offer for you to join the Value Exchange Leadership Mastermind. Claim it at the Book Holders section of the website.

26081047R00069

Made in the USA
San Bernardino, CA
15 February 2019